"True mastery is rare and precious—and Cheryl Fraser is truly a master of her subject. Written with a wonderful combination of simplicity and thoroughness, heart and intellect, and profundity and practicality, this is a phenomenal book on intimate sensuality, and equally excellent about communication skills and mindful awareness. Wow—a wonderful book."

—**Rick Hanson, PhD**, author of *Buddha's Brain*

"Sacred sex. Prolonged pleasure. Conscious climax. It's all part of using your sexual bliss energy to become an awakened lover, and Cheryl Fraser—a renowned Buddhist psychologist—is your guide to transcendent sex."

—**Ian Kerner**, sex therapist, and author of the *New York Times* bestseller, *She Comes First*

"Fraser asks pointedly, 'Why add the wisdom teachings of Buddhism to a book about passion?' Quite simply, because they work. *Buddha's Bedroom* folds the wisdom of Buddhist Dharma into the practicalities of love and sex to form a beautiful, thoughtful, and compassionate window into how 'old sex' can become new again. Fraser shares meditation exercises that she has used with countless couples, and teaches the reader how to awaken the passion that has been sleeping inside them.

This book is for anyone in a love relationship who wants to fall in love again (with the same person), and is willing to examine within themselves to discover that they possess the key to happiness. Fraser weaves in real stories from the couples who have walked the path with her, along with her own candid (and entertaining) experiences to illustrate to the reader how to bring Buddha back into the bedroom. I will recommend this book to my own clients (and friends!) and suggest that they clip each of the 'Love Bytes' and 'Buddha Bytes' scattered throughout the book!"

—**Lori A. Brotto, PhD**, registered psychologist, Canada research chair in women's sexual health, professor at the University of British Columbia, and author of *Better Sex Through Mindfulness*

"Sex and spirituality have been awkward bedfellows for as long as anyone can remember, and now we live in an era with plenty of chaos, confusion, misunderstanding, and contention about sexual roles and sexual acts. Here comes Cheryl Fraser to offer clarity, encouragement, and some very sound advice about how to ignite passion while remaining aware. She lets us know how we can dance and share with another—lovingly—and with the kind of mindfulness that doesn't drape a big, wet blanket over the proceedings."

—**Barry Boyce**, editor-in-chief of *Mindful* magazine

"Cheryl Fraser has done a remarkable job of combining her expertise as a sex therapist and relationship counselor with decades of Buddhist practice. *Buddha's Bedroom* guides readers to develop and sustain strong, healthy relationships, including passion and intimacy in the bedroom, through the power of mindfulness and applications of Buddha's teachings. At the same time, she performs an invaluable service to rapidly growing numbers of lay people embracing meditation and Buddhism as the path to a better life.

Buddhist teachings, traditionally the province of celibate monastics, can be confusing for lay practitioners when it comes to relationships, sensuality, and sexuality. Freedom from desire as a Buddhist goal seems inconsistent with sexuality in particular. However, Fraser does a beautiful job of demonstrating how the transient lust that relationships begin with can be transformed into an expression of love, compassion, and a manifestation of the Seven Factors of Awakening."

—**Culadasa (John Yates, PhD)**, spiritual director and chair
of Dharma Treasure Buddhist Sangha, and author of
The Mind Illuminated and *Brain Science for Greater Mindfulness*

"Can you be happy, passionate, and loving towards a mate of many years? Cheryl Fraser will make you a believer. Destined to be the definitive guide on mindful loving, this fresh, modern guide to intimacy harnesses wisdom from the ages. Everything you need to have a conscious, compassionate, and thrilling relationship is in this accessible and encouraging book. Cheryl Fraser has a vital message to share. Don't miss it!"

—**Maci Daye**, sex therapist, and creator of Passion and
     Presence® Mindful Sexuality Retreats

"Cheryl's book is a wonderful reminder of how the path is always within us. The simplicity and safety she creates around the topic of sexuality stems from her deep, personal practice combined with her clinical experience. Cheryl portrays the importance of the body's experience on our spiritual path. A recommended read!"

—**Nicole Daedone**, author of *Slow Sex*

"There is a belief many people have that once-passionate relationships eventually fizzle out over the long term and become routine and mundane. *Buddha's Bedroom* completely dispels that belief by inviting us to shift our view and be more intentionally mindful in how we connect with our partner and with ourselves. Cheryl Fraser provides many practical, exciting, and stimulating ways to uncover and rediscover the flames of passion that reside within all of us. This book is a 'must-read' for anyone in a committed relationship who desires to cultivate deeper intimacy and sexual passion through mindful loving."

—**Jennifer Nagel, MA, RCC**, individual, couples, and family
     therapist; director of training for the Satir Institute of the
     Pacific; and author of *Magic in the Muck*

"*Buddha's Bedroom* is a fascinating book that shows you how to fall in love all over again with the one you are with. If you think your relationship has become boring and the thrill is gone, you are in for a big surprise. According to Cheryl, the cure for your relationship issues are in your head, not your bed! Her extensive background as a psychologist, sex therapist, and Buddhist teacher give her unique insight into the real problems couples face. In her wise, humorous, relatable style, she leads us away from the soulmate trap and into the real love affair that is standing right in front of us."

—**Andrea Frank Henkart, MA**, best-selling author of
Cool Communication, international speaker, and certified
nutritional counselor

BUDDHA'S BEDROOM

THE
MINDFUL
LOVING PATH
TO SEXUAL
PASSION &
LIFELONG
INTIMACY

CHERYL FRASER, PhD

REVEAL PRESS

AN IMPRINT OF NEW HARBINGER PUBLICATIONS

Publisher's Note

This publication is designed to provide accurate and authoritative information in regard to the subject matter covered. It is sold with the understanding that the publisher is not engaged in rendering psychological, financial, legal, or other professional services. If expert assistance or counseling is needed, the services of a competent professional should be sought.

Distributed in Canada by Raincoast Books

Copyright © 2018 by Cheryl Fraser
    Reveal Press
    An imprint of New Harbinger Publications, Inc.
    5674 Shattuck Avenue
    Oakland, CA 94609
    www.newharbinger.com

Grateful acknowledgment is made to *Mindful* magazine, where excerpts from this book originally appeared.

Cover design by Amy Shoup; Acquired by Ryan Buresh; Edited by Gretel Hakanson

Library of Congress Cataloging-in-Publication Data on file

20 19 18

10 9 8 7 6 5 4 3 2 1   First Printing

This book is dedicated to ERH (1963–2016),

mentor, muse, lover, friend.

The last thing you said to me was, "Now go write your book."
So this one's for you, dearheart.

May you Snoopy dance forever in the place beyond words.

ASPIRATION

For the sake of all beings, may there be
wisdom, compassion, and mindful loving.

Contents

Foreword

By Jack Kornfield and Trudy Goodman

As a joyfully sexual couple, it is a pleasure for us to celebrate and support *Buddha's Bedroom* and the wisdom it contains. Buddha's own life included years in the pleasure palaces before his monastic celibacy. In this volume Cheryl Fraser puts these two together, offering the wisdom of Buddha's teachings tailored for the sexual life of laypeople.

Our culture is confused and torn about sexuality, dancing between repressive puritan ethics, like the reluctance to teach sexual education in schools, and widespread pornography and sexualized advertisements. Many religious traditions, including Buddhist monastic lineages, condemn or look askance at human sexuality, and sexuality has been a taboo topic in many dharma communities. Yet sexuality is also a doorway to the sacred, to intimacy, and to love. While Buddhist monastic tradition emphasizes celibacy and disparages sexuality, the Buddha also regularly acknowledged that wise householders get to enjoy the pleasure of the senses.

We long for love, for connection, for contact, and often for sexual fulfillment. Cheryl Fraser's long years as a Dharma practitioner and teacher as well as her equally long training in conscious sexuality make her an ideal, wise guide for this badly neglected terrain of meditation and sensuality.

In this book and in her work, Cheryl invites us to learn what she calls *mindful skills*—quieting and steadying the mind; becoming aware of bodily sensations; and learning how we hang on, how to let go, and how to channel meditative skill into passionate and playful sexual exploration, intimacy, and love. Cheryl expertly uses the foundational framework of the Buddha's eightfold path to formulate her eight steps on the *Path to Mindful Loving*. She shows us how to channel the skills of absorption into mutual awareness of sensation and skillful cultivation of loving kindness, compassion, joy, and equanimity.

We don't usually associate these four qualities with helping to rekindle sexual desire or to have great sex. Yet Cheryl shows us how these spiritual strengths are at the heart of loving sexuality and relationship. Her faith in the teachings of the Buddha, born of her deep practice experience, is communicated in her complete confidence in every couple's capacity to learn how to express love in more pleasurable and harmonious ways: to awaken, together.

Even when couples have succumbed to what she calls "Marriage Inc."—friendly, practical, long-term relationships devoid of sexual bliss and excitement—Cheryl is a cheerleader for partners to reclaim and discover a truly thrilling, sensuous connection to each other and to the beauty of life itself.

We acknowledge Cheryl's bravery in bringing Buddhist wisdom and meditative skills from their monastic, patriarchal context to the cultivation of happiness in sex and relationship. Training in mindfulness can nourish and intensify this dimension of our lives, too. It takes courage to surrender barriers to closeness and reveal our innermost vulnerability. With humor, relaxed ease, and playfulness, Cheryl teaches us ways to merge with sexual pleasure as a path to wonder, intimacy, openness, and awakening. In her words, "Mindful loving is about compassion and awareness, whether you are making love with your partner or making love with the world."

Preface

So there I was, looking for truth at the foot of the Himalayas, dodging soccer-playing little-boy monks as I chased the wicked monkey who had swiped my last bit of gourmet chocolate, and the big life-changing wisdom coming down on me was: Wow, I should have had less yak butter tea because it's bloody cold and I badly need to pee. And the outhouse is halfway down the rickety monastery staircase. Next to a pig. And I don't want to meditate or be enlightened. All I really want to do is get to the Tibetan-run Internet café so I can commune with the toe-curlingly wonderful man back home that I think I am falling in love with.

If that isn't a "How did I get here?" moment, I don't know what is. So, here's how: I'm a Buddhist sex therapist. I know, right? Not a career choice I saw up on the corkboard of life options when I was a kid. But I was kind of an odd kid. When I was four years old, I announced to my mom, "I like animals better than people because animals never hurt your feelings." Yup, relationships hurt, and as a little girl, I was already trying to figure out why. As I grew older, I continued to puzzle over why love affairs are difficult and why happiness seems elusive. So, I started seeking. I vowed I'd figure out what makes a great love relationship. And forty years later, I supposedly had the answers. I was a thriving psychologist, sex therapist, and "love expert." I designed a weekend love boot camp, teaching couples how to create passionate, loving relationships. I had a radio show giving love advice, wrote columns for magazines, and was even on TV. I was a bona fide relationship guru.

And I was single. And had been for ten years. I'd been in love often, married once, divorced once, and my hopeful heart had been broken over and over. In fact, I had given up on having the very thing I taught others to create—a spectacular relationship. Every day I helped couples connect with love, thrill, sexual play, and psychological depth. Then I went home to my seaside house with the steam shower built for two that had only been used by one and slept alone.

Yet, I did have a great love in my life, and his name was Buddha. And Buddha never broke my heart. He couldn't, because according to him, true happiness is not found in someone else. True happiness lies within. A happy heart was up to me. So, at the peak of my career as Dr. Cheryl, passion coach, I gave up on romance, dropped out of the spotlight, and married the Buddha. I spent several years alternating long silent meditation retreats with deep studies of the causes of inner happiness.

And for the first time in my life, I was truly happy. The longing in my heart was stilled. I didn't need a mate to feel fulfilled. I finally had it figured out. Or so I thought. Then, at the end of a deep, three-month tantric meditation retreat, I spoke with my meditation teacher. He asked me why I wasn't in a relationship. I choked on my jasmine tea. "Um …" I sputtered. "Because when I'm in a relationship, I'm miserable, I'm always wanting my partner to be different than he is, and I've finally discovered that I can be happy alone?" I offered. His calm dark eyes regarded me with amusement. And then he spoke. "Well, Cheryl, relationship is a very important part of the path."

The retreat ended, and I headed home to regular life. And to my great surprise, I met a guy. A handsome, thoughtful, deep, passionate guy. And I started to fall in love with him.

And then I left him behind and scampered off to India with my meditation teacher.

Which brings us to that aha moment in the Himalayas, my bursting bladder and I limping down a misty, monk-strewn mountainside, torn between the search for enlightenment and the man back home. Two paths, me in the middle, which do I choose? Nun or sex therapist, enlightenment or love, Buddha or my new sweetie? Suddenly I stopped chasing the monkey. I took a still, mindful breath of the chai tea and Tibetan incense-scented air. And I got it. My teacher's wise instructions cut through the confusion and the dualistic thinking. I quit hanging on to the belief that either Buddhism or relationship was the right path to happiness. I let go. The confusion cleared. And I saw the wisdom right in front of me. Love and awakening are not two separate paths. I didn't need to choose. And in that moment, the practice of *mindful loving* was born: Instead of believing love and happiness are somewhere over the horizon, we wake up to the beauty and connection of the present moment, with the person we are with, right now. Instead of seeking passion, we uncover the passion that resides inside us. Mindful loving is the teaching of love, sex, and enlightenment together—of bringing Buddha into the bedroom.

The Buddha Ruined
Love Songs

You have likely picked up this book because you want more passion than you currently have. You want to feel that "in love" feeling. You want love that is based in tenderness and daily routines but also has room for spontaneity, fun, and mind-blowing sex. You want to be happy forever—just like the love songs promise you can be. These are good things to want.

Like many people in long-term relationships, you may have some serious doubts about the possibility of ever feeling passion again. You remember what passion feels like—the delicious thrill of falling in love and the creative, fully absorbed sex—but it seems like that was a long time ago. Your love relationship may have faded into something more like a business than a romance. You may be caught in the day-to-day realities of running what I sometimes call Marriage Inc. You pick up groceries, pick up kids, and pick fights. You run through life and rarely slow down long enough to have fun together. You are friends, but not lovers. Sure, you have sex now and then, but the thrill and excitement are seriously lacking. Marriage Inc. is pretty much passion-free.

The Sun Under the Clouds of Marriage Inc.

Many couples that I see in my private practice and online courses assume that once the passion has gone out of the relationship, it's impossible to get it back, but this is absolutely not the case. There is an analogy that is often used in meditation teachings that I like to apply here. The happy, peaceful mind is described as being like the sun. The sun is always shining; however, we may or may not be able to see it. For example, if it is a dark, cloudy day, we feel like the sun is gone. But logic (and science) tell us that the sun is always there—even in the blackest night, somewhere the sun is doing its thing, shining brightly behind the clouds or darkness. The happy mind is also always present—even when you are in a sad mood. Once the clouds of negative emotion part, the happy mind shines through. Because it never left.

Your passion is the same way. Under the clouds of fatigue or lazy habits that go along with Marriage Inc., there is a shining sun filled with passion. And this passion resides inside you. The truth is, you won't find great love and passion outside of yourself. Great passion starts with you. Your task is to uncover the passion that is already there. Don't seek it from your mate—expecting them to act in a way that unleashes passion for you. Don't seek it in a new love affair. Seek it within your own heart and mind. Ultimately, despite what other relationship books say, you can only create great love with another person by working on your own head first. *Buddha's Bedroom* is about just that. In this book, I will show you how to renovate your love affair from the inside out—because love songs don't come true. But you can write a new song, once you understand what the Buddha figured out.

Why the Buddha Left His Wife

So, the Buddha ruined love songs for me. Before I met the Buddha, I thought a boyfriend would make me happy. Forever. Deep inside me there was a longing, a visceral hunger, for love with a capital L—love that would make life worth living, love that would be amazing and romantic. I really thought that I would find someone special and that we would live happily ever after. And then I did. I found love, great love, when I was sixteen. He was a logger, an artist, and a cat lover. He had spiky black hair and eyes the color of the ocean on a bright spring afternoon. He was funny, kind, and passionate. He silkscreened special Ramones tee shirts that we wore to their concert. My boyfriend was my most trusted ally and my best friend. He was also my first lover—together we discovered how tender, passionate, and beautiful sex could be. It was everything I wanted in a love relationship. Capital L love, indeed. So why wasn't I happy ever after? Yes, our relationship brought moments of great happiness. Yes, love was wonderful. But a call inside me—sort of like that of a kitten scratching gently at the closed bedroom door to say I am here, pay attention to me, I want to come in—kept demanding my attention. There was something else that was the answer to life-long happiness, and it wasn't Prince Charming. And that's where Prince Siddhartha—the Buddha—comes in.

The Buddha was a man in search of an answer to the happiness question too. As a young man, a wealthy prince, he lived like a rock star would today. His every whim was catered to; his every need was met. Eventually, he married a beautiful princess, and they had a son. Things were all going according to plan for Prince Siddhartha's parents, who wanted him to be a leader and a businessman, not a seeker of the truth. They wanted the kitten scratching on his soul-door to be drowned out by the sounds of singing minstrels and the coos of his progeny. So, they did not want him to see the ugly side of life. Much like a rock star is sheltered from reality inside a private jet, well protected from the horrors of an economy-class middle seat beside the toilets, the future Buddha's folks kept him within the palace grounds, hoping he would never see what it was like to be poor, sick, or old. They wanted to shelter him from the truth. Because the truth is that life involves some suffering, no matter whom you marry or how rich you are.

But then, one day, Prince Siddhartha convinced a servant to take him on a life-changing joyride outside the sheltering palace walls, and he saw things he had never seen before. He saw lepers with oozing sores, crying piteously by the side of the road. He saw old people bent over in pain, spines curved like cruel candy canes. He saw a dead body for the very first time. He saw the fundamental truth of life—that nothing lasts forever. He saw ... reality. And reality grabbed him and shook him like a border collie does a stuffed squeaky squirrel. In what I imagine was a terrifying moment of clarity, the prince saw through the lie of his own outwardly perfect life. He saw that wealth and health and a good marriage do not last. He began to question everything. And he realized that happily ever after is in fact a big illusion.

But then the prince saw a holy man, a wanderer who had turned his back on the worldly life. The holy man looked serene and absolutely content—peaceful without a palace. This man had no possessions, no home, no wife, no baby. Barefoot, clad only in a cotton wrap, carrying only a broken branch as a staff, his face glowed with warmth and happiness. *How can this be?* thought the prince.

As the story goes, the prince returned to the palace, shaken into existential angst. He looked around at the beauty and riches and saw them for what they really are—temporary dams against the torrent of truth. Then he slipped into the bedroom where his wife was asleep, their babe in her arms. He watched the rise and fall of the sheet as his loved ones breathed in and out. The prince's heart chilled when he realized his own son would get sick, would get old, would end up a corpse. Reality, once seen, could not be unseen— the reality that this life, even the most wonderful, rock star life, is also filled with suffering. Then he remembered the holy man. And he realized he could slip under those sheets and pretend life was fine, or he could face the truth.

He vowed he would find an answer to the problem of suffering. An answer to the question, *Why are we not happier?* He realized that the answer was not to be found in riches or relationships. Love is not the answer, and love songs don't come true. He saw that the answer had to be sought inside his own mind. And so, Prince Siddhartha kissed his slumbering son, stroked the cheek of his beautiful bride, and walked out—on his way to becoming the Buddha.

Love Is Not the Answer

The prince headed out on his quest. He was absolutely determined to discover the cause of suffering and the way to end suffering. He searched and practiced and trained with the greatest meditation masters. He did extreme cleanse diets—at one point he was down to eating one grain of rice a day. He trained his mind so he could get into profound meditation states, dwelling for days in bliss and joy and orgasmic pleasure. Yet even those bliss states were not the answer, because they had a beginning and an end. Hanging on to a bliss state was just a temporary fix, no different than hanging on to a new chocolate bar, car, or lover, and expecting that to make us happy forever. Sublime meditation states don't change reality or end suffering altogether.

Finally, after many years of complete dedication, he sat down under a bodhi tree and vowed he would not get up until he discovered how to be free of inner unhappiness. And he did. At the base of that tree, after facing his mind demons, after fiercely penetrating into the nature of reality, and after uncovering the shining sun of awareness under the clouds of confusion, he got it. The answer doesn't lie outside; it lies within. The prince figured out how to be happy all the time, no matter what the circumstance. He saw the path to freedom, peace, and compassion. And in this moment of realization, he became enlightened. He was completely free of all mental pain, all anxiety, all judgment. He was a Buddha: a fully awake human being, with full happiness in his mind, all the time. He was, in essence, love—unconditional, expansive, complete, awakened love.

Wow. So, what happened next? As the story goes, our former rock star prince, now a simple holy man with a world-changing discovery, got up and went for a walk. And he ran into some of his old meditation buddies. They saw immediately that he had figured it out. They fell at his feet and begged him to share what he knew. And he did. He boiled his radical discovery—his discovery of awakened love—down to the Four Noble Truths, or four facts of life. And it rocked his friends' world. They finally understood the root cause of their suffering and the way to fix it. When I heard these facts of life, I finally understood why is staying in love is so hard. He taught that love is a sickness and the only cure is to stop believing that love will set us free. There is no soulmate. Love is not the answer. And that's how the Buddha ruined love songs.

The Buddha saw that if we accept things the way they are and stop trying to make them be the way we want them to be, we are happy. So instead of spending your life fiddling with the outer—repainting your bedroom, going on a vacation, trying to make your spouse attend the opera with you—he pointed to the importance of fiddling with the inner, training your mind and heart toward happiness and away from distress. In essence, things outside us can't be controlled, and they don't last forever. Happiness—in life and in love—lies within.

The Dharma of Love and Sex

The basic premise of *Buddha's Bedroom* is that relationship techniques are never enough. The only way to truly transform your relationship, to create thrill and passion, to fall in love all over again, is to renovate from the inside out. First, work on your own mind. Then, and only then, will you be successful in creating connection, thrill, and blissful sex with your partner. Let's start with some meditation and Buddhism terms you will need to know. Consider this your introduction to the Dharma of love and sex.

Buddha. The word "Buddha" means "the Awakened One." For those of you unfamiliar with Buddhism, chapter 2 gives a crash course in Buddhist teachings and how they relate to love relationships. For now, I just want to clue you in to the main terms and definitions. So, to be a Buddha means to be a person free from suffering. A Buddha's mind is clear, loving, and compassionate, and so too are a Buddha's words and actions.

Dharma. *Dharma* is a Sanskrit term that means many things, but the definition that best suits us is that dharma means wise teachings. So, the dharma of love and sex refers to the true nature of love and sex and the teaching, or way, of wisdom in relationships. When we add the word "Buddha" to the word "dharma," we get the word Buddha-Dharma. This means the teachings of awakening.

Awakening. *Awakening* means having a mind that is free of suffering. It means seeing things as they really are, without confusion. Imagine your mind being completely free of any negative emotion or incorrect assumptions. No anger, no sadness, no irritation, no anxiety. Imagine your mind being filled with calm, happiness, feelings of friendliness, and care and compassion for all. That is an awake mind. In terms of your relationship, imagine looking at your partner with love, interest, and acceptance. Imagine no judgment or irritation or disappointment. Imagine passion and sensuality that feels new and exciting. That would be how an *awakened lover* feels. And you can aspire to that.

Mindfulness. *Mindfulness* as a word and an idea is thrown around a lot these days, sometimes accurately and sometimes less so. From the perspective of Buddhism, mindfulness means being aware of what is actually happening in the present moment, without stories or interpretations. Mindfulness involves calmly noticing and accepting your thoughts and feelings as they occur, without believing them to have a substantive reality.

Mindfulness is the practice of observing your direct experience of what is actually happening right here and right now. For example, as you read this paragraph, are you mindful? Let's find out. What are you currently focused on? There are many things happening in your direct experience right now. Some of them are in the forefront of your attention—perhaps the words themselves, the concepts you derive from the words, the low hum of the cat purring in your lap. Other sensations and perceptions are in the periphery of your attention: you are vaguely aware of them, but they are not on center stage. However, you can become aware of them if you try. For example, perhaps there is a clock ticking quietly on the wall. Can you hear it? Before I asked you to pay attention to that sound, you were not consciously aware of it. But now you have deliberately invited it into your direct experience. In other words, you became *mindful* of the ticking clock sound by paying attention. Mindfulness is that attention itself, the act of noticing the experience of hearing a tick, not the ticking clock itself.

Meditation. There are many types of meditation both within the Buddhist tradition and across other traditions, both spiritual and secular. We will work with two forms. First, there's *mindfulness meditation*. Some of you will be familiar with this practice, and it will be new to others. Mindfulness meditation, in its simplest form, is the practice of choosing an object to deliberately focus your attention on. Often the chosen meditation object is the breath. As you saw in the previous paragraphs, attention and awareness are fluid things. You can be aware of many things at once. Some will be in the forefront of your attention; others, in the near or far background. With mindfulness practice, you choose to try to keep the sensations of breathing in and breathing out at the forefront, and to allow everything else—thoughts, body sensations, sounds, smells, tastes, sights—to fade into the background of awareness. You remain nonjudgmental and accept what arises, whether you like it or not. Inevitably, your attention will rebel, and instead of staying focused on the breath, attention will chase after a thought or the itchy feeling in your right elbow. At that point, you perform the active part of meditation—you deliberately refocus your attention on the current breath. You attempt to let go of the distraction—and it is called a distraction, by the way, because it interferes with your chosen pursuit of placing the breath sensations, nothing else, in the forefront of your attention. You attempt to be mindful of breath and allow everything else—traffic noise, thoughts about what to have for breakfast—to just continue on about you on its own. You avoid making up stories and daydreaming. You simply have the direct experience of what your breath feels like, here and now.

A second form of Buddhist meditation is called *open awareness meditation*. In this form, instead of choosing one thing, say the breath, to focus on, you develop the ability to rest comfortably in meditation without preference. You "open up" your awareness and allow all the sounds, smells, tastes, physical sensations, sights, and thoughts to simply be present. Here, it is as though your attention is a vast lake, upon which all the five senses and the activities of mind are reflected. When thoughts appear, you don't chase them. They just appear, like ripples on the lake appear around a fallen leaf, and then they still again. Meanwhile, your mind is the lake. The lake doesn't react to the leaf, the ripples, or even the alligator. It just rests in its essential lake nature. With open awareness, you can rest in the still, peaceful curiosity of your open, calm mind. That's a great place from which to engage with your partner.

Love dharma. So, how does all of this apply to love, sex, and happy relationships? Why add the wisdom teachings of Buddhism to a book about passion? Quite simply, because they work. By applying the dharma teachings of mindfulness and awakening to your love relationship, you can create freedom from suffering and be happy in love. You can stop longing for something else, or someone else, and directly experience the beauty that simply is, here and now, with the person you are with. Great passion can be uncovered, and meditation can help. According to the dharma, great love and sex are all in your head, even if they end up in your bed. As you saw, the Buddha worked on his mind until he was fully awake. He was filled with peace and happiness and passion. In *Buddha's Bedroom*, you will work on your mind so you can become an awakened lover.

Awakened lover. To be an awakened lover, you uncover and awaken the passion within you, the sun under the clouds. It means you truly inhabit the beauty and sensuality of the present moment—you love with mindfulness. When you love mindfully, passion will follow. Because passion is not just about having great sex. Deep, profound passion is based on being awake, fully present with a calm mind and a loving heart. Passion is about being in the moment where your senses are alive and sparkling and your mind rests more easily in loving thoughts. As you delight in the present moment, sensual experiences are intensified. Sex becomes both explosive and transcendent. When you truly connect, you will shiver with the sensation of fingertips grazing wrist and feel fascinated with your sweetheart even after all these years. And this translates into better relationship skills. As you awaken your inner lover, you will find it becomes easier to think, speak, and act with awareness and kindness. This in turn uncovers the passion within you and ignites passion between you and your beloved. When you let go of your preconceived ideas, you can listen with your heart and wisdom instead of your fears and ego. When you can focus on the sensation of tongue on tongue, you experience this kiss with the intensity of the kisses you had in the beginning. When you listen like this and kiss like this, you are practicing being an awakened lover.

Train Your Mind and Become an Awakened Lover

It turns out great love and great sex are all in your head, and passion resides within you. You can uncover great passion, and then share it with your partner. This book shows you how. I draw from both couples therapy and Buddhist teachings to give you practical skills that create freshness and curiosity with the person you have been with all this time. This touch on your thigh, this coffee and croissant together, can be intensely interesting, fun, and sexy. In other words, what was old can become new again. Your passion seemed to die because you forgot how to be lovers. The excitement may have faded, but you can bring it back because passion never left; it just clouded over for a while. By combining meditation and marriage techniques, I will show you how to play together both romantically and sexually. As you will see, mindfulness will help you uncover the passion under the clouds of Marriage Inc. You will begin to see your partner with new eyes and touch them as though you have never touched before, and your passion will be contagious. Buddhist philosophy can radically change how you approach your beloved and your relationship. I present the Buddhist teachings in the form of what I dub the *mindful loving path*, which is comprised of eight aspects of mind and action that, when cultivated, will transform your love affair. Utilizing what I call *mindful skills*, you will learn mindfulness techniques that will help you to train your mind and become a much better lover. This is the "Buddha" part of *Buddha's Bedroom*.

By the way, this teaching is not meant to imply that it is completely up to you to work on your mind and uncover passion and that your mate doesn't need to work on him- or herself. Of course, I'm not saying that. No, what I am saying is that ultimately, no matter what your mate does, it is your reaction that determines whether you are happy or unhappy in the relationship. I've discovered in my own relationship, and in my work with thousands of couples, that if you work on your mind, your relationship will improve. But if you both work on your minds, your relationship happiness will improve a lot. So, this book is written for both of you. Love is a hard gig, and to thrive in love on a day-to-day basis, you definitely need some tools and ideas to work on together, in addition to your own mind training. Your partner is not the cause of your misery, but they can be a great part of the cure. So, in addition to showing you how to work on your own mind and attitude, I will give the two of you concrete strategies to work on together as a couple.

The "bedroom" part of *Buddha's Bedroom* includes what I call *love skills*, which are designed to help you speak and act with love and awareness. Building a foundation of intimate connection helps to uncover the latent passion within you and to manifest this passion with your partner. Love skills can create deep connection and sensuality that surpass even the romance the two of you had in the good old days of falling in lust and love. I present the love teachings in the form of what I dub the *passion triangle*: three key aspects of your love relationship that need to be explored and strengthened in order for you to create lifelong, sustainable passion.

To really apply the ideas in *Buddha's Bedroom*, you need to do two things. One, train your own mind with the teachings of Buddhist psychology and mindfulness. Two, work on relationship skills both on your own and with your sweetie. You will then develop deeper intimate communication, create spontaneity and playfulness, and explore the erotic together. When you combine couples' skills with mindfulness, you can create connected intimacy, a sense of thrill (that "in love" feeling), and sparkling sensuality that ranges from gentle lovemaking to wild raw sex and tantric orgasm. That is what *Buddha's Bedroom* is all about. When you accept the challenge to employ these techniques in your own relationship, you begin the practice of uncovering the passion within you and becoming an awakened lover.

Are you ready to walk this path? To uncover and become passion and awaken the lover within? Join me and learn to love with presence and to make love with sizzling awareness. No matter how long you've been together or how deeply your passion is buried under the clouds of Marriage Inc., you can rewrite your love story, mindfully. Then together, you can cultivate passion that lasts a lifetime.

How to Use This Book

Many people say they want a great relationship, great sex, and great passion. But talk is cheap. You, however, are different. You want love, happiness, and passion enough that you're willing to take the time to read this book. The first thing I have to say is congratulations. You've taken the first step toward creating passion that lasts a lifetime. In this book, I offer you the culminated learning from decades of study of relationships, sexuality, and meditation. I offer these teachings as clearly as I can. I aspire to make them understandable, entertaining, relatable, and effective. I aim to teach you the path of mindful loving and how to create a strong passion triangle. But I cannot walk the path for you. I can only give you the map. And maybe I will even pack you a little picnic complete with chocolate body paint and a bottle of bubbly. But you will need to set your intention to change your old patterns and make new ones. And then you must do the work. For if passion happened all on its own, you'd already be basking in a great love relationship and you would be naked with your sweetheart right now instead of reading a book.

What I want you to do is take the lessons and techniques out of these pages and apply them to your own life and relationship. Really give them a good try. Set aside time to practice the skills offered here in a way that will give you the most benefit. If you already have an established meditation practice and some knowledge of Buddhist teachings, great. If not, start right where you are. Begin a meditation practice using the mindfulness practices taught in this book. If you already have experience with various relationship techniques, great. If not, the exercises in this book will teach you how to think about, speak to, and act toward your mate with love, curiosity, and interest. If you have a rich and rewarding sex life, great. If not, trust that you can create passion. But if you skip ahead to the sex chapters (and who can blame you?), please note that without a basis in mindfulness practice, deep sexual bliss experiences will be difficult, and without a good, communicative, healthy relationship, sex may not happen at all. In other words, mind skills, relationship skills, and sexuality skills interrelate. That's why *Buddha's Bedroom* is about all three.

This book is written primarily for people in a love relationship. All of the techniques and teachings apply to heterosexual and alternative couples—all that's required is two (or more) people who love each other and want to learn to become more intimate and sexually passionate. I recommend that you read the exercises, try them, and talk about them with your partner. And if there are some bits that don't really apply to you or don't seem to fit well to what you've already learned in your life so far, then let them fall by the wayside. But don't quit too soon. The words "I know this already" can stop you from seeing something familiar in a new way. Sometimes you will want to skip an exercise or idea, and it is actually the very thing you need—a technique that could lead to a breakthrough. But don't worry, you are not alone. This book is only the beginning. Visit http://www.drcherylfraser.com and sign up to receive weekly Love Bytes and Buddha Bytes via email, access guided meditations, and participate in live coaching sessions with me and the community of other awakening lovers. And most of all, be easy on yourself and on your partner. Change takes time. But you can do it. I know you can. Because the love and passion you seek are already slumbering inside you. All you have to do is wake them up.

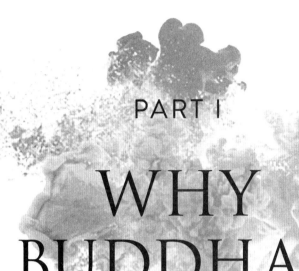

PART I

WHY BUDDHA'S BEDROOM?

CHAPTER 1

Sex, Love, and Meditation

If you are like the majority of couples in a long-term relationship, you wish you could feel as alive, and romantic, and yes, horny, as you did in the beginning of your love affair. But you don't really think it is possible to feel that way again. You may even believe passion is a game for the young, or worse, for the desperate middle-aged who chase after their passionate past by having a fling with a young stud or filly. After all, "mature love" is comfortable, right? You love your sweetheart. You feel affection for them. You raise the kids well and have a good time on your annual vacation. Things are fine. But "fine" is not passionate. And as a sex and relationship psychologist, I am here to tell you that "fine" is not enough. Great relationships do exist. And they are not an accident. Sure, there are a few couples who seem to have it going on naturally—but do you really think they came by it easily?

You probably know a long-term couple who seem to have an exceptional love relationship. I know I do. Bob and Janet have a passionate love affair, even after twenty-six years of marriage. His hand rests on her shoulder while he tells a story about their trip to India. They speak in glowing terms about each other. Janet shares, with obvious pride, that Bob was just awarded a medal in recognition of the hot breakfast program he spearheaded in the poorest schools in our district. With a conspiratorial shared glance, Bob confesses that their sex life is better than it ever was: "In fact, she looked so good tonight I kissed her in our garage, and before you know it, we were back in the den having a quickie on the couch!"

I'm not surprised to hear it. Because Bob and Janet demonstrate the qualities of both mindfulness and passion.

Passion Is a Teachable Skill

Bob and Janet appear to be one of the few lucky couples who won the passion lottery. But it is wrong to think that those rare couples with long-term passion are simply lucky. Having great passion between you and your partner is not based on luck. Long-term passion is a teachable skill. I know that sounds counterintuitive. After all, passion is spontaneous. It is unpredictable. Sometimes you feel passion for the wrong person at the wrong time. Can you really feel passion again for the person you have slept beside for twenty-six years? Yes. I am here to tell you that passion is 100 percent possible for you and your partner. Because passion never left. Passion is not dead. It is only slumbering. You can awaken the lover within you if you are willing to try.

Bob and Janet did not come by their long-term passion easily. They lost their second child at birth. After this devastating event, Bob coped by throwing himself into his career. He and Janet argued almost every day. Their sex life was badly affected. They rarely made love, and when they did, it was more about obligation than connection. Eventually, when Janet told her husband she wanted to separate so she could explore happiness and passion elsewhere, Bob fell apart. The grief he'd been bottling up for three years poured out. Janet saw the tender, emotional, passionate man she used to know. Together, they began the slow process of uncovering the passion under the clouds of grief and overwork and neglect. Eventually, they built a relationship that is the envy of all who know them.

When you find yourself envying another couple and wishing you had what they seem to have, take heart—because you can. Remember, just like the sun is always shining, your passion is always shining too, even when it is obscured by the clouds of irritation, fatigue, and routine. Passion is a renewable resource. Your own mind is the key to uncovering passion.

First, uncover passion. Train in mindfulness and meditation, see the present moment as it is, and dissolve the clouds between you and love. Realize happiness is in your head. That's the Buddha part. Then, become passion. Take action to create a profound, intimate, and sexual relationship with your beloved. That's the bedroom part.

Relationships Are Dukkha

When it comes to love, you don't need the wisdom of the Buddha to tell you what you already know: Relationships are difficult. Falling in love doesn't last. Despite what movies would have us think, there is no happily ever after. In Buddhist terms, the truth is that relationships are *dukkha*. "Dukkha" is a Pali word—the language of the Buddha's time—and it means "unsatisfactory." Sometimes the word is translated to mean "suffering." Romantic relationships will always include some suffering and dissatisfaction. In other words, love hurts.

We all want to be happy. We fall in love, and it feels so fantastic at first. We believe love will last forever and that we will always have passion, connection, and fun together. We believe we have cracked the code and found the answer to the happiness question. And then things change, and love goes from feeling wonderful to feeling rotten at least some of the time. No matter how wonderful the falling-in-love phase was, you eventually hit some big roadblocks to happiness. Try as you might to make your partner change, you fail. Even the good relationships have way too much disappointment and annoyance, and the bad ones have abuse and betrayals. It turns out that falling in love is easy, but staying in love is a hard gig. Love is absolutely wonderful. But love is also full of dissatisfaction. If you think of couples you know well, how many of them are radiantly happy in their relationship? If love were the final answer to happiness, wouldn't we all be a lot happier?

Love dissatisfaction is a real thing. This is a simple truth with profound implications. Because if love doesn't make us happy, why do we keep thinking it should? Instead of looking to love itself, or our mate, to make us happy, we need to look inside ourselves and uncover the happiness, and the passion, within. Now I can almost hear you protest, "Sure. Dr. Cheryl, I'll work on myself, but hey, I am miserable because of my partner. They are the one that needs to change." Well, I'm here to tell you that your partner is not the problem.

The Problem Is in Your Head, Not Your Bed

So, the problem is dissatisfaction in love. Coming up, I'll explain in more detail how Buddhist teachings diagnose the cause of your love dissatisfaction and show you how you can cure it. But for now, I think we can agree that you are unhappy with at least some aspects of your love relationship. Maybe you feel as though your sex life is in a rut or that you have grown apart. Maybe you'd like to feel more connection, fun, and romance with your partner; to communicate better about tough topics; or to experience passion and eroticism, like you used to. Whatever your desire, the solution to the love dissatisfaction problem is always the same. According to the Buddha, you need to change your mental patterns, not your partner. In essence, "Change your mind, not your mate," needs to be your motto.

Your partner is not the problem. Your mind is the problem. When you find yourself unhappy in love, what is actually occurring? Well, usually you are unhappy because your partner is failing to do something you want them to do. Perhaps they forgot to say, "I love you madly, and you look hot in your mom jeans, baby." Or they are doing something you don't want them to do. Maybe they are picking their toenails when you are trying to watch *Game of Thrones*. So, they are making you unhappy, right?

Wrong. You are making yourself unhappy. You are unhappy because of your own mind. Happiness is possible in this very moment, even if your sweetie is picking their toenails. All you need to do is let happiness be. Now, don't misunderstand me, I'm not blaming you. I know how difficult relationships can be, and how unhappy our minds can make us. What I'm saying is that *you already possess everything you need to be happy in each and every moment.* Your perspective and attitude toward whatever is happening are the keys to whether you are happy or unhappy, not the thing that's happening itself. This may sound easier said than done, but it applies to your love relationship, and for that matter, your whole life.

The realization that happiness is inside of you is the best Valentine's Day gift ever. Because it means that you, not your partner, are in control of your relationship happiness. Once you realize that your mind is the key to passion, you can uncover the thrill you think you've lost. You can be happy, you can be in love, you can be in a great relationship, and the solution does not lie in your partner; it lies in you. Change your mind, and your relationship will change. Or, more accurately, your relationship *toward* your relationship will change, for it is how you react to things that determine whether you feel happy or miserable.

Here's an example: Yesterday, my friend Joe went to collect his work truck, and it was not where it had been left the night before. Now, imagine you are standing in the parking lot, looking at the spot where your truck should be, and feeling confused. Then you realize the truck must have been stolen. You feel anxious. *How will I get to work? Will the boss fire me? I'm an idiot for leaving the keys hidden by the gas cap.* Next you feel angry. *Who did this to me? A punk kid?* Then you feel defeated. *Things never work out for me.* After experiencing this roller coaster of emotions, Joe called me, and the first words out of his mouth were, "Well, this is going to be a lousy morning." He then told me about the missing truck. So, was Joe correct? Was it a lousy morning? Well, in a way, yes. If Joe's mind *decided* it was going to be a lousy morning, it was indeed a lousy morning. But if Joe's mind *decided* it was going to be a great morning, it would be a great morning—a great morning with a stolen truck in the middle of it, which is what I pointed out to him. Joe's mind made it a good morning or a lousy morning—not the presence or absence of the truck, or the actions of whoever took it.

That's Buddhism in a nutshell. You are happy, or not happy, in the mind. So, when it comes to love, you are also happy, or not happy, in the mind. This is earth-shattering information because it means that in order to be happy in your relationship, your partner doesn't need to change at all. Your mind does.

This is where mindfulness and Buddhism come in. One half of the teachings in this book are to help you change your mind. The other half show you how to bring that new head into bed, so to speak—how to apply your new mind-set to creating connection, romance, and great sex with your beloved. You will learn to change your love affair and create relationship happiness from the inside out. And you will do that by becoming mindful, both in meditation and in love.

MINDFUL SKILL: Mindfulness of Body Sensations

I suggest you begin a daily mindfulness practice if you do not already have one. Begin with ten minutes a day and gradually expand to thirty minutes a day. As you will see throughout this book, creating a base of mindfulness is very helpful. It can provide a ballast when you are caught up in unhelpful emotions or stories and support you to apply mindful loving techniques. Here is a great starting meditation. This simple yet profound mindfulness practice will become important when you begin the practice of bringing mindfulness to touching your partner. You can read it over and then practice it. For additional support, visit http://www.drcherylfraser.com/buddhasbedroom. There, you will find several audio guided meditations, including this one, that will assist you in mastering the material in this book. There is also a teaching on meditation posture you can review.

Find a comfortable place to sit, either in a chair or cross-legged on a meditation cushion. Adjust your posture so your body is alert and upright, yet relaxed. Allow your eyes to close. As you begin to settle into the meditation session, at first simply let your mind roam as it wishes. Various sense and mind objects will draw your attention—perhaps a sound, next the sensation of an itchy nose, and then a thought about getting groceries this afternoon. This is to be expected. No problem.

After a few minutes, begin to invite your attention to focus on body sensations. How do you do this? It is indeed an invitation. You invite your attention to focus a little bit more on body sensations—the gurgling feeling in your stomach, the warmth of the sunlight on your elbow, the movement of the chest as it rises on the inhale and falls on the exhale. Focus less on the other things your mind is concurrently aware of—the birdsong, the idea for a weekend getaway that just arose in the mind, the scent of the peonies in the vase next to you.

It is as though you are at a cocktail party and you are focusing your attention on a fascinating conversation with an old friend. At that party, you invite your attention to focus in on your friend's words, and you allow the other distractions—the laughter of the other guests, the clinking of glasses, the blur of movement and color as people dance in the living room—to fade into the periphery of your awareness. Play with that right now. Allow the busy "cocktail party" of ideas, emotions, sounds, scents, and all other distractions to fade into the background of your awareness. In the foreground, pay attention to the "conversation" you are selecting—in this case, the feel of any and all body sensations.

Allow yourself to rest in this experience. Many things are happening in and around you, but you are choosing to narrow your focus to body sensations. When the attention is grabbed by something else, a thought or sound, no problem. Just attempt to let go of that distraction and refocus on the body. This is just like at the party. If someone drops a platter of glasses, your attention will be grabbed away from your friend's words temporarily and will focus on the clattering sounds. But you then are able to refocus your attention on your interesting discussion.

Relax as best you are able into the experience of sensations in the body. You may allow the attention to roam throughout the body, perhaps first noticing and really experiencing the feeling of your tingling foot, next noticing the sensation of your thighs pressing against the chair, and then feeling your tongue on the roof of your mouth. Really experience body and touch sensations. Explore with gentle curiosity and interest. As you allow other distractions to subside into the background, you may experience body sensations more intensely. The more mindful you become, the more acutely you will feel the direct experience of touch sensation.

Explore in this manner for approximately twenty minutes. Observe what it feels like to pay close attention to a body sensation. What is it like to allow the mind to settle down, at least a bit, and really feel the breeze on your cheek?

When you are ready to end your mindfulness of body sensations meditation, open your eyes.

Don't Seek Passion, Become Passion

When people complain to me that that they want more passion in their relationship, they tend to say some of the following things: "I wish my partner was more romantic." "Oh, if only I could have more passion in my life." "Our sex life is either boring or nonexistent. Where'd the passion go?" The problem is that each of these common ways of thinking about passion takes you out of the driver's seat. You are cast as passive when passion itself is fundamentally active. Everyone wants passion, but many of us have no clue how to go about cultivating it—outside of waiting around and worrying because it's not happening all by itself. Very rarely do people ask: What can I do to experience more passion in my relationship? How can I help my partner feel sexy and passionate again? What action can I take to fix this?

Like many of my clients and students, maybe you have simply given up and accepted a passionless relationship. Perhaps you blame your spouse, scolding them for the lack of sex or romance and fervently wishing they would act more passionately toward you, or you are ever hopeful that passion will simply reemerge next Tuesday. But let's be honest. Can you realistically expect passion to suddenly sweep you up like it did when you were falling in love? If you are waiting for passion to simply happen, or you feel the passion exists outside you, you are doomed. The spontaneous, lusty passion of falling in love is based on a mix of hormones and illusion. It's a powerful chemical and emotional cocktail that by definition is time limited. That thrilling feeling is created by oxytocin, serotonin, dopamine, and adrenaline stewed together with hopes, and dreams, and yes, love songs. It often has little to do with reality. In fact, being "madly in love" mimics the brain chemistry seen in obsessive-compulsive disorder. And it passes. After the chase, the pursuit of the love object, the chemistry of early passion calms down. After all, the chase is finished, the prize has been won, no more effort is required. Unfortunately, this means that when you have been together for a while, you can't just wait around hoping that those early, intense, and natural feelings of passion for your spouse will spontaneously reappear. Your chemistry has changed to that of contentment, not excitement and lust.

You are the key to passion in your relationship. The first lesson is that becoming passion is active. It is you, creating your love affair and being responsible for your relationship happiness. In my view, the term "love life" needs to be rewritten a wee bit. I like to add the letter R and turn your love life into "lover life." Neuroscience research indicates that word choice and thoughts have an effect on physiology and emotions, and the word "lover" takes you from wishing for a great love life into action and doing. In other words, as a lover, you create the very thing you want. You become passion.

And rather than seeking to be "in love," how about seeking to be a great lover? Too often when you are frustrated with your relationship, you make it about what you are not getting. And wanting is painful. (More about that when we get to the Buddha's four facts of life and how to get enlightened—or at the very least, how to be happy in love.) Observe that when you are stuck in wanting something from your partner, it is difficult to act in a loving manner. Perhaps you are longing for your partner to take you on a romantic date. You want them to be spontaneous and do all the planning and sweep you off your feet. Well, how about you take action instead and plan the fabulous date yourself? Make it special, and make sure you choose something your sweetheart will love as much as you do—perhaps Mexican food at the new salsa place, followed by a dance lesson and a sensual night of moving your bodies in tandem, or a burger and beer followed by the latest action flick. When you take action and create good circumstances, you relieve the painful wanting inside you, and instead you create the very connection and contentment you crave. Concentrate on *being* a lover, not on *getting* the love you think you need.

When you commit to wanting a phenomenal relationship filled with love, connection, and sizzle, you uncover that buried passion within you and then cultivate the skills necessary to manifest and sustain passion with your partner. I invite you to become the very thing you want. In order to become passion, you must take responsibility for your own passion and get active about your lover life. You must take command and stop waiting around for something, or someone, to "make you feel passionate." It is time to become passion and create a passionate relationship from the inside out.

LOVE SKILL: A Great Lover Is ...

I'd like you to participate in a thought experiment. Think about what it takes to be a great lover. Close your eyes for a few moments and make a mental list of the qualities a "great lover" possesses. What came up? When I ask that question to couples at my Awakened Lover weekends or during my online couples course, it's remarkable what the answers are. Over and over, the words that come up are ones like intimacy, respect, humor, passion, imagination, trust, joy, friendship, kindness. Someone said, "A great lover smells good." Another said, "They care about your happiness, both inside and outside of bed." Very rarely do people say a great lover is super skilled at sex or a great lover can perform Kama Sutra number 47. Because being a great lover is about so much more than sexual technique.

Don't get me wrong, I think sexual skill is an important aspect of being a lover. Later in this book we will absolutely talk about sensuality and sexuality and teach some erotic techniques. But *lover* is a fairly encompassing concept. It involves friendship and intimacy. It involves trust and respect. It involves sizzle and sexuality and passion. It involves gentleness. It involves rawness and fire. It involves a variety of things. Once you have created a mental list, write it down. Then discuss your list with your lover, and invite them to share their list with you. As you move through this book, review your list and expand it. Later you will revisit this list and apply it to your own relationship.

Love Bytes

♥ Passion is 100 percent possible for you and your partner. Don't settle for "fine."

♥ Great relationships take effort. Rather than waiting for passion, vow to become passion.

♥ An awakened lover brings curiosity and presence to their mind and to their beloved. It turns out great love and great sex start with you.

♥ By changing your attitude toward your mate, you can fall in love all over again.

Buddha Bytes

🪷 If love doesn't make us happy forever, why do we keep thinking it should?

🪷 Your current partner is not the problem. The problem is in your head, not your bed.

🪷 Love is not the answer. Inner happiness is. You are happy, or not happy, in your mind. That's Buddhism in a nutshell.

🪷 Change your mind, and your relationship will change. Create a passionate relationship from the inside out.

CHAPTER 2

Buddha's Cure for Lovesickness

The Buddha's four facts of life gave me the answer to the question that years of university programs in psychology and couples therapy could not—namely, how can two people actually live happily ever after? By training your mind, you can uncover the passion within and feel love for your partner no matter what is happening. You can be happy during the good times, and you can even be happy during the bad times. This is where dharma teaching is so revolutionary. You can remain loving through the weddings and betrayals and kissing and farting and all the rest of the real-life relationship issues that the original happily ever after storytellers neglected to warn you about.

The Four Facts of Life and Love

What the Buddha discovered under the bodhi tree, and then taught for the rest of his life, is simple and yet earth-shatteringly profound. The Buddha discovered how we can indeed be happy in life. He boiled his discoveries down to four facts, and they are:

1. Sometimes life hurts.

2. There is a reason life hurts, and it is not what you think.

3. Once you know the real cause of your pain, the cure is obvious.

4. Happiness is an inside job.

The sections that follow explain these facts in more detail and then show you how to apply each of them to your love relationship. Thanks to the Buddha, you can learn not only why you are unhappy in love, but also how to fix it. You can uncover the passion and awakened love that is always present in both you and your partner—and then walk the path of mindful loving, together.

First Fact: Sometimes Life Hurts

You know that sometimes life hurts. Have you figured out why? The reason is actually very simple: Things change all the time. And sometimes things change in ways we do not want. And that hurts.

The Buddha taught this as the truth of impermanence: the simple truth that things are ever changing. Right now, if you are sipping an oolong tea while you read this chapter, things are changing all around you. The tea is cooling. The light on the page, in the room, and outside is shifting. The sounds inside your home and outside in nature quiver and dance. Your skin is shedding cells, your heart is beating, and leaves are budding or falling from the trees around you. Your mind is alternating between calm and anxiety, interest and boredom, happiness and sadness. Everything changes.

The law of averages—and your own life experience so far—indicates that some changes will be experienced as positive and others as negative. In other words, you like some changes, and you dislike others. For example, imagine that after you finish reading this chapter, you decide to drive to town. When get to your car, one of two scenarios plays out. In scenario one, someone has left a bouquet of flowers on the hood. In scenario two, someone has left a bag of dog poop on the hood. Most likely, you have a reaction. To what? To a change. You'd probably find the first scenario to be a positive change, and so you'd have a positive reaction. "Yay! Flowers! I feel happy!" But chances are that you'd have a negative reaction to the doggie bag. "Darn it! Poop! I feel angry!"

The Buddha's revolutionary realization was this: *we suffer not because things change in and of themselves, but because we want things to change in certain ways.* And nowhere is this truth easier to spot than in our love relationship. As long as we believe we can ignore the truth of impermanence, we will be love-sick.

Lovesickness: Nothing Lasts Forever

The first fact of life states that love is like a sickness because although it brings great joy, it also brings some very unpleasant symptoms. Love is great, and sometimes love hurts like crazy. You don't need me to tell you that; you've been in love before. So, let's look a little more closely at what our experience of love is and how the Buddha's facts of life explain how and why love hurts.

We seek love for a complex bunch of reasons. We want to feel connected and avoid loneliness. We want the pleasure of sexual contact. We want someone we can take care of and who will take care of us. We want to have kids, a home, a family. We want to share the bills. We want to fill a psychological void left by an imperfect childhood (and there is no other kind). We want to feel pretty, handsome, important, admired. We want to show our peers that we, too, are worthy of love. We want to travel the world with another adventurer. We want someone to make us tea in the morning. We seek emotional and financial stability. And we want someone to grow old with, to sit beside in our favorite chair on our favorite porch as we gaze into the twilight of our life. That's the plan.

We seek love, then we find love, and for a while, we are happy. If only those feelings would last forever. But they don't. Enter the first fact of life: everything changes. Our best-laid love plans fall apart. And that truth of impermanence, the truth of change, can make you unhappy. Remember, things don't always change in the way you want them to—and this includes the person you love. What happens when your sweetheart makes you cocoa every morning for years, and then one day they don't? Do you feel hurt by them? By this change? Over and over, even in a good relationship, love involves some dissatisfaction and discomfort. So, it is fair to say that love hurts. Inevitably, love or our lover sometimes makes us sad, angry, frustrated, and even devastated. Not all the time, of course. Love is also filled with wonder, joy, and simple contentments. Don't misinterpret these facts of life—they are not dour or fatalistic. They are, simply, realistic. They are facts. A great scientist simply reports what is. So did the Buddha. And so am I.

Second Fact: There Is a Reason Life Hurts, and It Is Not What You Think

Fact number two points out that the cause of our sickness, our unhappiness, is hanging on. We cling to wanting things to be a certain way. In other words, we fight reality. Reality is not the problem. So, whether your car is covered with flowers or poop, reality is just, well, reality. Whether you feel happy or angry has nothing to do with what is sitting on your car hood; it has everything to do with your reaction to reality. The suffering is created by your mind's reaction, not by the events themselves. *Bad luck doesn't make you unhappy; you do.*

Now let's apply this to love. When I first heard the second fact of life and realized there was one simple cause for all relationship misery, it blew my mind. We are sick, it hurts, and we don't know why. We keep blindly trying to fix our lovesickness, but we can't because we don't understand what causes us to be sick. It's extraordinarily painful. What a relief that the Buddha explained the cause of our suffering. In fact, I have a student who was so excited when she got the meaning of the second fact of life that she spun around three times in her office chair. And that is an appropriate reaction. Because once you know the cause, you can do something about it.

The Cause of Lovesickness: Hanging on Hurts

When your spouse points out that you may have gained a few pounds, they hurt you, right? Well, maybe not. According to this second fact, it is your inability to accept reality that is the problem. If you are annoyed with your sweetie for the extra pounds comment, it is because you are hanging on to wanting things to be different than they actually are. You want to be slim, or you want a partner who thinks before they speak. And that's pointless. It won't cure you. Because things just are as they are. You have thickened around the middle. Your body changed. Your partner's observation is just that, an observation. Your sweetheart is not responsible for your reaction to what they thought was a harmless comment, and therefore, they didn't hurt you. Your mind hurt you. I know, I know, this can be hard to accept at first. Be gentle with yourself and simply take it under advisement for now.

Here's another example of how your mind causes lovesickness. Your partner was supposed to pick up cat food on their way home, but they forgot. That is reality. Then it gets interesting. You feel annoyed, perhaps even angry, or hurt. Maybe you start thinking that you can never rely on your partner. Yet the simple reality is that your sweetie forgot to stop by the store. You can like it or not like it. Either way, the cat food is not here.

So, what's that cause of your misery? The cat food? Obviously not. Your partner? Less obviously not, but still, not. Your own ideas and expectations? Now we are getting somewhere.

When your mate or your relationship isn't "making you happy," the actual problem is that *you* are not making you happy. You are hanging on to something, trying to change reality. In this case, your mind wants a partner who always remembers to do what you ask them to do. But guess what? That is not the partner you got.

This is the part where you spin around in your chair. Go ahead, I'll wait. Because this is great news! It means you can be happy no matter what your partner does. There is a simple, identifiable cause for your lovesickness. And it's not that you married the wrong person. Your partner doesn't hurt you. Your mind hurts you because you are trying to bend reality to your will and script a better reality, or rather, one that you like better.

All that misery, all that lovesickness, is caused by a single thing: hanging on.

What would happen if you just let go?

LOVE SKILL: What Are You Hanging on To?

If you are upset or unhappy with your partner, there is a cause, and that cause is not actually your partner. So, for this exercise, identify a moment of lovesickness and then identify the cause. Ask yourself three questions:

1. What do I believe to be the cause of my current unhappiness?

2. What am I hanging on to?

3. How do I want reality to be different than it is?

Here is an example from my own relationship. This morning I awoke feeling peaceful and happy. I smiled as I listened to the singing birds. Then I heard the revving of a garbage truck. I turned toward the man I love and snapped, "Arg! You forgot to take the garbage out *again,* didn't you? You're so unreliable!" I jumped out of bed, grabbed the mutts, and headed for the beach. I glowered at the overflowing trash cans, blaming them for not strolling to the curb by themselves. I was unhappy. I was annoyed with my partner. But what was causing my suffering? I believed my guy was the cause. What was I hanging on to? I was hanging on to wanting the garbage to be collected and wanting my man to have "done his chores." But that wasn't reality. The reality was simple: my beloved forgot to put out the trash. That's all. My mind made me lovesick because I wanted something different. When I asked myself these questions, I was able to see how pointless my wanting was. My heart softened, and I felt love, instead of annoyance.

Now, bring to mind something that happened between you and your partner this week that upset you. Then ask yourself the same questions. Really examine the true cause of your suffering. How does it affect your thoughts about your mate when you hang on to wanting things to be different? See if you can feel the tension, the unpleasant emotions, that are created by hanging on.

As you practice this, over time, you will begin to truly experience how your own mind is creating a lot of your unhappiness. And eventually, you will become much more skilled at letting go and allowing yourself to be happy despite the circumstances. After all, I can have a wonderful morning whether or not my sweetie took the garbage out, simply by taking the garbage out of my own mind.

Third Fact: Once You Know the Real Cause of Your Pain, the Cure Is Obvious

If the cause of our sickness, our unhappiness, our suffering, is hanging on, how do we cure it? This is not a trick question. The answer is obvious: Stop hanging on. Let go.

In this moment, if you are unhappy, it is because you are hanging on to something. You want things to be *different than they actually are.* But clinging to wanting things to be different is futile. Things are as they are. Fact of life number three says let go of your clinging, and happiness will arise. So, if your lover forgets your birthday and you let go of wanting breakfast in bed and a romantic birthday card, you will not suffer. The minute you let go, suffering stops. This third truth is elegant, simple, and beautiful.

The Cure: Let Go and Be Happy in Love

Let go of your hanging on, and you can be happy in love forever. That is how you cure lovesickness. Here's an example: A client I saw yesterday feels irritated when her man forgets to check the live mousetrap in the crawl space. She imagines poor Mickey dead of starvation in his cruelty-free trap, remnants of peanut butter on his wilted whiskers. Does being upset make her partner less forgetful? Nope. If she wants to be happy, she can simply let go of hanging on. I asked her how she'd feel if she could shake her head at her partner's relaxed, go-with-the-flow style, a style so unlike her own. I pointed out that hanging on to wanting things to be different is a dumb way to find happiness. Letting go and simply being happy, connected, and in love, right in this moment, is a brilliant cure for relationship ills.

But let's get real. This simple cure—let go and accept reality—is darn hard to do. Over and over again, you find yourself unhappy because of something your partner did or didn't do. You hang on, you hurt, then you repeat, and that is lovesickness. Luckily, pain is a great motivator. None of us like hurting. We like to be happy, so once we understand the facts of life and love, we try to let go more often. And sometimes we succeed. Letting go of minor annoyances probably feels doable. I bet you can work on letting go of the need for your partner to iron that shirt before they wear it. Hey, maybe the rumpled, unkempt look is in at their office. But what about the big things, the ones that come with large chunks of pain and suffering? Well, the big hurts have exactly the same cause as the small ones. Perhaps you feel bolts of fear when you imagine your partner might leave you one day. You are hanging on to your partner's promise that you'll stay together forever. That clinging can cause terror and jealousy and huge suffering. Remember, everything changes. In fact, your partner will leave you one day, if not by choice, then by death do you part. Love doesn't hurt. Your mind hurts. Love just is.

And it's not your fault that letting go is so very difficult. We humans are deeply conditioned by a life of patterns, a life of believing that we can change things to be how we want them to be. You have been trying to control reality and make the world and your sweetie do what you want them to do for a very long time. So please be easy on yourself. We are talking about a radical rethinking here. It takes a lot of work to learn to let go more easily and more often. It takes practice and dedication to become an awakened lover and to learn to be happy in love, just as it is. It takes time to cure lovesickness. Thankfully, there is a prescription.

MINDFUL SKILL: A Meditation on Letting Go

Begin by settling into a comfortable sitting position. Bring your attention to the feeling of your breath by placing your attention on your chest. Notice the gentle rising of your chest on the inhale and the falling of your chest on the exhale. Notice whether your heart center feels open or tight, connected or disconnected. Practice mindful attention to the sensations of breathing into and out from your chest, your heart. Practice this way for several minutes, inviting the mind and body to settle down a little.

Next, bring to mind the relationship event you identified in the previous exercise. For me, it was the garbage can incident and my subsequent annoyance. As you think about the event, notice any sensations in your body or mind that arise. Perhaps there is a tightening in your chest or an emotional feeling of sadness, anxiety, or irritation. Don't try to change your experience; just bring mindful attention to it. Don't judge yourself or the feelings; just observe them with curiosity, as though you are watching someone in a movie who is feeling those feelings. If the feelings get too uncomfortable, return to focusing on the sensation of the breath rising and falling in your chest. Take a break from experiencing your distress and regroup.

Next, when you are ready, ask yourself what you are hanging on to. If you were the author of this story, how would you want the story to go? Get clear on what you wanted the ending to be.

Then notice that you are hanging on to wanting something that did not happen, something other than reality. Allow yourself to rest with that awareness, the awareness that things unfolded the way they did, not the way you wish they had. Are you able to hold that truth gently? Reality just is, but sometimes you very much want a different reality. Explore how it feels to want something different than what happened, to grasp, to cling. Notice if that wanting is comfortable or uncomfortable. Notice what it feels like to hang on.

Then, as much as you are able, pretend you can let go of the desire for things to be different, for the story to have a different ending. For me, I would practice letting go of wanting my sweetie to have taken the garbage out. I would really try to *experience* what it feels like when I let go of that wanting. What if I just choose to be fine with the truth? To have it be no big deal? What does that feel like in my emotions, my body, my heart?

Practice going back and forth between holding on to the ending you wanted, like you are grasping with your fist, and feeling what it is like to let go, opening your fingers and exposing your palm, as you try to gently accept the ending that actually happened. Grasping, releasing. Closing, opening. Suffering, ceasing to suffer. Feeling less love, feeling more love.

After you have explored this experience of hanging on and letting go for some time, allow all of that thinking to fade away. Bring your attention to the chest, to the heart center. Focus gently on the physical sensations of breathing in and breathing out. Notice if your chest feels any different than when you began. And when you are ready, open your eyes.

Fourth Fact: Happiness Is an Inside Job

In order to be free from suffering, you have to change the way you think about happiness and how you react to the many changes life delivers. It turns out happiness is an inside job. And not an easy job. It is going to take effort to become an awakened lover, to be a mini-Buddha in your own relationship. And the Buddha seems to have known how difficult it would be for us to change the way we think, react, and behave. So, he gave us a path—the Noble Eightfold Path—to help us learn to be happy in life and love from the inside out, no matter what cards are dealt. This fourth fact of life offers eight areas of study to help us train our thoughts, words, and actions to create happiness, peace, and wisdom in our mind and in our life. When I apply the Buddha's facts of life specifically to love relationships, I call these the eight qualities of "mindful loving." Think of the *mindful loving path* like an awakened lover training course, a prescription for love, happiness, and passion.

The Prescription for Happily Ever After

The Buddha's first three facts of life teach you the cause and the cure for your unhappiness—the what and the why. The fourth fact gives you the how. To recover from lovesickness, you need to apply what the Buddha prescribed. Let go of hanging on, accept reality instead of fighting reality, and train your mind to be calm and loving no matter what is happening around you. That means you stay happy whether or not your partner takes you for a kayak ride to a hidden chalet for date night or forgets completely and shows up at the stroke of midnight, filthy and unaware like a post-pumpkin Cinderella, after spending what was supposed to be date night drywalling their uncle's garage. In order to do this, to become an awakened lover, you need to revise how you *view* your partner and identify what your *intentions* for your relationship are. In doing so, you create more relationship wisdom. This in turn produces more integrity in your *actions, speech,* and *relationship skills*; you become a more loving and connected partner. By training in *mindfulness* and *concentration,* and making *loving effort,* you increase your awareness, sexual pleasure, and passion. These are the eight qualities of mindful loving.

In the next chapter, we will take a closer look at the path of mindful loving and how you can bring the four facts of life and the teachings of couples and sex therapy together. It is time to follow the path to a great relationship. It is time to bring Buddha into the bedroom.

Love Bytes

- ♥ Love is great. But sometimes love is painful and difficult. Why? Because things change.

- ♥ Good news! You can be happy no matter what your partner does.

- ♥ Lovesickness is a curable condition. The cause is hanging on. Let go and let love flourish.

- ♥ The prescription for happily ever after is the mindful loving path—an awakened lover training course.

Buddha Bytes

- ☸ If you train your mind, you can feel love and passion no matter what is happening.

- ☸ Reality doesn't hurt; your mind hurts. Let go of wanting things to be different, and happiness will arise.

- ☸ You can create lasting passion by learning to love your mate and your relationship as they are.

- ☸ Your spouse cannot make you happy. Happiness is an inside job.

CHAPTER 3

How to Bring Buddha into the Bedroom

So, what's actually in Buddha's bedroom? A triangle and a path.

The triangle is the *passion triangle*. The passion triangle illustrates the three key ingredients of passion: thrill, intimacy, and sensuality. This is the bedroom part—the relationship work, the practices that create emotional connection between you and your beloved that show you how to skillfully communicate, manage conflict, and awaken your desire and sexuality.

The path, on the other hand, is what I call the *mindful loving path*. The mindful loving path applies the wisdom of the Dharma and the Eightfold Path to love and relationship. This is the Buddha part—the inner work of training your mind and uncovering the passion under the clouds. It can be helpful to remember that, ultimately, great love is all in your head. Until you access the passion inside you and can tap into it regularly, you will find it impossible to sustain connection and passion between you and your partner over the long haul.

In this chapter, I'll teach you how to combine the passion triangle and the mindful loving path to help you become a more awakened lover. When you join the inner work of training your mind with the outer work of developing loving behavior in the emotional and sensual realm, you unleash the natural love and passion within. Then, you can create connection and sexual bliss that last a lifetime. You can be more like a Buddha in the bedroom and beyond.

The Passion Triangle

The passion triangle is the model I use to teach couples how to create lifelong romantic and sexual passion. You want your relationship to be built on a strong, reliable foundation. My friend Ian, who is an engineer, told me that the equilateral triangle is a highly stable structure on which can be built huge, beautiful buildings. It has three equal sides, supporting each other. If I'm looking to build the ultimate passionate relationship, a love affair filled with joy, intensity, loyalty, and desire, a relationship that becomes deeper and sexier as time goes on, then I want to build that on a very strong foundation.

The three components of the passion triangle are:

Thrill: The ineffable sense of excitement, interest, and attraction to your partner that you experienced when you fell in love but that often fades.

Intimacy: A deep sense of knowing and being known that develops over time through shared vulnerabilities and deepening emotional connection.

Sensuality: The spectrum of romantic, erotic, and sexual connection between two people, from hand-holding to wild sexual delight.

If you are like most couples, you are strong in some areas of the triangle and weak in others. But if you want sustainable passion and connection, you need all three sides to be strong. Now, let's begin by examining each side of the passion triangle a little more deeply.

Thrill

Imagine you are seated at a table in your favorite restaurant, waiting for your partner. You've just returned from a week away on business, and you have missed them terribly. As you sit there scanning the sidewalk through the window, searching for them among the crush of people hurrying home from work, you feel an edge of excitement. There is an aroused quality as you seek your beloved's face. And then you spot them, and there is a small rush of thrill in your body and emotions. It's unsettling in a delicious way. That's what I'm talking about in terms of *thrill*.

Do you feel that titillating anticipation of thrill these days? Or are you more likely to watch cat videos on your phone than scan the restaurant for the welcome face of the one you have chosen to spend your life with?

If you rarely, or never, feel thrill anymore, take heart. It's a big old myth that the thrill can't last forever. That is simply not true. As an awakened lover, you will learn that even though the thrill does fade for a whole lot of couples, it doesn't need to be that way for you. It's not easy, but you can uncover the thrill that you used to feel. Thrill is always there, shining brightly underneath the routines and familiarity of Marriage Inc. You will learn to get mindful and see your partner—and the world—with fresh eyes. Then, what is old becomes new again, in this very moment. And *this* one as well. You will fall in love all over again, with the one you are with.

Intimacy

When I use the word "intimacy," I'm talking about deep emotional connectedness and loving friendship. True intimacy is a sense of being deeply known by the other. To be known is to share your secrets, to reveal your best, and also to reveal the parts of yourself you are not proud of. In a deeply intimate relationship, you learn to trust that your partner will love and accept you no matter what. You don't need to hide the fact that you have vulnerabilities and fears, and that you're not perfect. In the depth of intimacy, you can be seen for everything you are, dark and light. You don't have to play a role or pretend.

Real intimacy develops over time and through many shared life experiences. I am not talking about the initial false sense of intimacy you can feel with a stranger. For example, my friend Lucia had a fantastic first date with a man. They shared tapas and wine and talked and touched and laughed and then walked by the ocean. She said, "I feel like I've known him all my life." Except she hadn't. She had known him for four hours. That early sense of connection, while it feels wonderful, is not the real thing. Your love-song-laden heart projects fantasies onto the person standing in front of you. This creates an intoxicating sense of closeness. The problem is projection obscures reality. What you are feeling is not real intimacy, and it doesn't last. After the lust chemicals die down, the work of real intimacy begins. Intimate partners share multiple joys and sorrows. They are in it, to quote the traditional marriage vows, "for better and worse, richer and poorer." As an awakened lover, you realize your partner is not responsible for your happiness. You make efforts to deepen and refresh the intimate connection between you by paying mindful and loving attention to your beloved as though you are still infatuated. You learn to see your imperfect partner and your imperfect relationship with clarity—and love them more than ever.

Sensuality

Sensuality. What a delicious, fantastic, rich word. For the purpose of the passion triangle, when I say "sensuality," I mean the entire spectrum of sensual and sexual energy that you feel within you and exchange with your partner. There are untold possible sensual delights. However, if you are like many people in a relationship, your sexual spectrum has narrowed to only a few colors. Perhaps in the beginning, you made love all over the house and nibbled on each other's toes. And then your thrill slowed down. Life got busy, and Marriage Inc. took over. You know, the routine, tag-team partnership of two jobs, two kids, two busy people, and one neglected lover life. Your sex life became predictable, infrequent, or nonexistent. But you can change that. These teachings of the passion triangle and the mindful loving path will help you expand your sensual repertoire.

As an awakened lover, you connect with your five physical senses and the sixth sense, which is your mind, in new and powerfully erotic ways in the service of sensuality. You explore new ways of connecting with sensual pleasure and joy, whether that's intertwining your fingers while you take the dogs for a walk in the woods or sharing an urgent, fast orgasm in the spare room while your family has dessert downstairs. You learn that desire starts in the mind as well as the body. You inhale the scent of your partner's neck and linger as you savor the taste of their skin. Holding eye contact brings erotic intensity, and you revel in the sound of their sighs as you massage their feet. You delight in the sensual pleasure of touch, from the shiver of fingertips caressing the back of a hand to the neglected art of kissing for hours. Then, once you hit the bedroom, your sensual exploration will range from the sweetest, soul-shaking lovemaking to the hottest, raw sex to tantric transcendence. There are almost limitless ways that two hearts, minds, and bodies can connect in the sensual realm. That is sensuality. This sensuality can be present at orgasm and just as importantly when you are holding hands in the woods, and at every moment you spend together or apart.

LOVE SKILL: Rate Your Passion Triangle

Where is your triangle currently strong, and where is it weak? Rate yourself on thrill, intimacy, and sensuality on a scale of 0 to 10, with 0 being the complete absence of that quality and 10 being the highest possible level of that quality. For example, a 2 in sensuality might mean you rarely or never have sex, you don't kiss or cuddle much at all, but you do hold hands at the movies. Your sensuality is currently weak. A 7 in intimacy might mean you feel close and connected to your partner, you feel a lot of love and comfort, but you argue more than you want to, so there is room for improvement.

This simple rating is meant to be a quick status update about the current state of your relationship. Note that your passion triangle can fluctuate a great deal. If you've had a fun, relaxed weekend sailing with friends, on Monday morning you might rate intimacy at a 9 because you enjoyed each other's company and got along wonderfully, thrill at a 5 because sailing was a new adventure and you enjoyed watching your partner learn to trim a sail, and sensuality at a 6 because you kissed more than usual and made love on Sunday morning. However, that weekend might have been unusual, and you'd rate your typical triangle as sensuality 4, intimacy 5, and thrill 2.

Try not to get hung up on these numbers. This exercise is intended to get you thinking about the three key elements of passion. Once you become more familiar with rating your passion elements, you will be able to focus on the areas that are weak and apply the techniques in this book to strengthen each side and keep it strong.

Balance Your Triangle for Great Love and Sex

To have a fantastic long-term sexual and romantic relationship, all three sides of the passion triangle are vital. When they are out of balance, your relationship will suffer. You can end up with love but no lust, or excitement without connection. If you're best friends and intimate confidants but don't cultivate thrill and sensuality, you won't have an exciting sex life—you might have pleasantly pedestrian sex, but it's not going to be passionate. As the brilliant therapist Esther Perel notes, too much intimacy kills desire. Or, if your intimacy is harmed by conflicts and criticism, you won't feel thrilled when your partner walks into the room, and you won't want to make love with them. If you have lots of sensuality but low intimacy—you can only connect through sex, but you hold parts of your heart and mind back, unsure whether you can be accepted fully—you won't be able to explore the true depths and breadths of your entire sexual self. It takes intimacy to make soul-shaking love and to trust that you can play in the dark depths of your raw desire. Yet when all three sides of the passion triangle are strong—*wow*. You feel accepted and known, *and* you feel alive and intrigued, *and* you are able to reveal your deepest sexual desires. You can let go of inhibitions while remaining deeply connected to your lover and explore your sensual self with freedom and abandon within the safety of love and intimacy.

Janine and Ed sought me out because they haven't had sex in four months. They describe themselves as "best friends." They text each other frequently throughout the day, sharing updates about kids and chores. When he has a work deadline, she brings a meatloaf sandwich to the office, and when she has menstrual cramps, he snuggles beside her flannel-clad body. But they are friends, not lovers—they have too much intimacy and very little sensuality or thrill. Janine rarely wears anything other than yoga pants, and Ed is more likely to kiss the baby than his wife. Not only is their sexual life at a complete halt, but they don't even flirt with each other. It's time for them to take action and cultivate more thrill and sensuality. I coach them to send each other one sexy or romantic text a day. Janine tells Ed that she misses the guy who used to sweep her off for surprise dates—the manly, romantic lover under the sweet, gentle daddy. He says he misses seeing her in feminine clothes, looking pretty and sexy. Together they come up with a plan for Ed to court her again—he will plan dates; she will dress up. They pledge to make one night a month an erotic date—they wanted to explore combining emotional intimacy with deep sexual desires. Over time, with commitment, effort, and a sense of play, this couple begins to strengthen the sensuality and thrill in their marriage and uncover the passion under the passivity. They learn that good things come in threes.

The Mindful Loving Path

You want to be happy in love, right? You want to cure your lovesickness. The Buddha's prescription includes eight ways you can train your mind and actions so you can increase happiness, reduce suffering, and uncover thrill, intimacy, and sensuality. A triangle, a Buddha, and a path. This may sound like a lot, but everyone would be an awakened lover if it were easy, right? Each of the following eight chapters takes one piece of the mindful loving path and shows you how it can ignite your lover life, one step at a time.

Loving View

Loving view helps develop relationship wisdom. How you view the world determines your expectations of how the world should be. And it certainly determines how you see your mate and your relationship. For example, do you believe love lasts forever and that it is your partner's job to make you happy? Reality clearly teaches that is not the case, so perhaps you need to change how you are looking at love and passion. Loving view helps you cultivate a new perspective on how to be happy in your relationship, see your partner more clearly, and become determined to love them better. Loving view helps you believe in and then uncover the passion within you.

Loving Intention

So, you want more love and passion. How can you turn that desire into a reality? By setting *loving intention*. Let's say you'd like to go to Paris next spring. That longing is insubstantial—no matter how much you daydream, it is just a desire. In order to get to Paris, you must take that desire and turn it into an intention. An intention is the bridge between the idea and the action you take. Once you intend to go to Paris, you will start to compare flight plans and research hotels with a view of benevolent gargoyles. If your intention is strong enough, *mon ami*, soon you'll actually be in Paris. Everything you do successfully starts with an intention. And becoming passion is no different. To create the relationship you desire, start setting loving intentions.

Loving Action

The woman on my office couch is angry: "He never tells me I look pretty. It's like he doesn't even care about me." Her husband, a man of few words, looks defeated. I gently help him articulate. "I may not say a lot, but that doesn't mean I don't feel a lot. Of course I care." Then I hit the gold hidden under his silence. He reveals that every morning he takes her shoes from the cold garage and places them in the cozy kitchen. "I don't want her to have to put her feet into cold shoes," he says with a shy smile. Hearing that, his wife softens. Sometimes, actions speak louder than words. Act like a lover, a best friend, and as though your mate is the most precious thing in your world. That's *loving action*.

Loving Speech

"I love you." "I slept with someone else." "I do." "I can't take it anymore." Words matter. And how you use them in your love relationship matters even more. Kind speech is the glue that strengthens and maintains your bond of love and affection. Skillful words can help you negotiate the most painful conflicts and heal the deepest wounds. Learn to speak from your heart and listen with love—for communication is a two-way street. *Loving speech* is a profound practice.

Loving Livelihood

In the path of mindful loving, let's consider your relationship as a *loving livelihood*. Just like doing meaningful work with carefulness and integrity helps create a peaceful heart and happy mind, creating a meaningful connection with your mate, treating them with care, and behaving with integrity within your bond create a peaceful relationship and a happy partner. Work overtime to be the best lover you can be. Love may not pay the bills, but it makes life worth living. That's loving livelihood.

Loving Mindfulness

You will hear a lot about mindfulness over the course of this book because it's critical to all eight aspects of mindful loving. *Loving mindfulness* involves paying attention. It involves being aware of your thoughts and emotions, other people, and how you relate to them. It helps you be a great partner—and not just out of bed. Loving mindfulness *definitely* includes mindful sex. When you can pull your thoughts away from worries or fantasy and connect with your lover in the here and now, you will feel a new depth of sexual desire. When you make love from a place of deep intimate connection and focus, your body, mind, and emotions come together in ecstasy. That's loving mindfulness in bed.

Loving Effort

"I never thought our sex life would change," she wailed. "We used to light candles, drink champagne in bed, and spend hours making love in all sorts of positions. Now we don't even kick the dog off the bed." I've had hundreds of couples say a variation of the same thing. It takes *loving effort* to keep your passion alive. But don't be discouraged. Every other skill you've developed took effort, too. That's not a bad thing. And for goodness sake, don't tell me that love should be easy or that needing to make effort in your sex life is not romantic. Consciously directing your life energy toward cultivating exceptional connection and sizzling sexuality is the most romantic thing I can imagine. Great sex is not an accident. Want to be an awakened lover? Make some loving effort.

Loving Concentration

Can you recall a previous erotic experience—one that was really intense? Perhaps it was lying on the downstairs couch with your teenage girlfriend or boyfriend, kissing for hours, nothing else in the world existing other than their lips and tongue. Or maybe it was the first time that someone you were wildly attracted to slowly slid their hand up your bare thigh. What were the qualities of those experiences? You were very absorbed. Your senses were focused in one place. Distractions—the hum of a lawn mower, the uncomfortable position of your arm—faded into the background. Now imagine being able to enter that state when you want to, able to make love with that intensity and flow. By practicing *loving concentration*, you'll learn to dissolve into transcendent bliss together. How do you think your partner will feel about that?

MINDFUL SKILL: Your Lover List

When you walk the path of mindful loving, it's important to know where you hope to end up. Set your priorities. Some people spend more energy thinking about what features they want in their new car than they do when they shop for a mate. Each of us is a bit different in terms of what we value in love and relationship. List the top ten things that you really want in your deep, passionate lover relationship. If they're open to it, ask your partner to do the same. What are your passion priorities? Do you want deep emotional connection? Do you want clear, kind communication? Do you want a wild, lusty sexual life? Do you want a wonderful and committed co-parent? Do you want a footloose and fancy-free travel companion? You likely have dozens of things you want in your relationship, but narrow it to the top ten. Write down your list of priorities. Then ponder them. See what you truly, deeply want. If you're working through this activity together, share your list with your partner, and learn about their list. Notice where your needs and desires overlap and where they diverge.

Now remember, an awakened lover is not just in it for themselves. They know they must act to become the passion they want. As you study your sweetheart's list, start asking yourself what you can do to make your partner happier. Pick one or two actions that you can work on this month. If your partner wants more connected conversation, make a vow to yourself to schedule thirty minutes each week, without interruptions, to listen and talk with them. If your partner wants a physically affectionate relationship, be aware of that and make a conscious effort to hug them more, to kiss them good-bye, or to make love at least twice a week.

Be kind to yourself. This exercise is just to get you thinking about what you can do for your sweetie, rather than focusing on what you need and want from them. But it is unlikely that this preliminary exercise will create radical changes right away. If it were that easy to change things and be much happier in your love relationship, you'd have done it. Changing conditioned patterns is not easy. You can do it, bit by bit, but it takes some time and effort. As you move through this book together, you will train your mind toward compassion and thoughtfulness. Let these lover lists, yours and your partner's, start to build a map for what the two of you plan to create in your passionate lover relationship. This is the preliminary work of becoming an awakened lover, a lover who takes action and strives to bring happiness and joy to their beloved, as well as to themselves.

Becoming an awakened lover means shifting the fundamental way you look at your partner and approach your love affair. It means taking responsibility for your own happiness and unleashing passion over and over, creating the flow and connection that define great love and spectacular sex. To become an awakened lover, commit to changing your mind, not your spouse, by working with the passion triangle and the mindful loving path over the course of this book. Let's go.

Love Bytes

- How balanced is your passion triangle? You need thrill, intimacy, and sensuality for a lifelong passionate relationship.

- "The thrill can't last forever" is a big myth. Sure it can. It just needs a little help.

- True intimacy develops over time, and it predicts marital success. Can you be vulnerable and open with the one you love?

- Sensuality encompasses the entire spectrum of sensual and sexual energy, from hand-holding to wild sex.

Buddha Bytes

- The mindful loving path applies the Buddha's wisdom to love and relationship. It's the prescription for happily ever after.

- Understand the true source of relationship happiness and set your intention to become an awakened lover.

- To be happy in love, you need to take loving action. Turn your desire into reality.

- Mindfulness is key to being a great lover—desire, passion, and pleasure are here-and-now experiences.

PART II

THRILL

THE MINDFUL
LOVING PATH

CHAPTER 4

Loving View

Don't Change Your Mate, Change Your Mind

The first step in the mindful loving path is to cultivate a loving view, or wise perspective. How you view your sweetie will powerfully determine the success and harmony of your relationship—and whether you keep the thrill alive. Let's say you see your chosen mate as an ever-changing phenomenon filled with surprises. With that view, you think about them often throughout the day, shaking your head with a smile of gratitude that you get to spend your life alongside such a fascinating person. You even feel a bit of thrill when they walk through the door. But if you think it is your partner's job to make you happy, you see them as a means to an end. You don't think about them much when you are apart, unless they do something particularly nice for you or something you dislike. And you sigh because they "don't make you feel passion" anymore. But remember, your mind is the key to your happiness in life and in love—not your mate. If you want to uncover the mind of thrill, don't change what you are looking at—*change how you are looking at it.* Thrill and passion are alive and well under the clouds of familiarity. It's not time for a new lover; it's time for a new view.

Loving view is, to a large extent, about unlearning. You learned that your partner was supposed to be the key to your happiness. You learned that love would last forever and that a house, kids, and fulfilling work were the meaning of life. But the four facts of life say that is not the case—that the key to being happy, or unhappy, is in your mind, not in your relationship. Hanging on to wanting things to be different leads to suffering. Letting go and accepting the truth of the present moment as it is, whether you like it or not, stops your suffering. Loving view is all about seeing things, and your mate, the way they are, even when they are not the way you want them to be.

There is a reason loving view is the first step the Buddha emphasized on the path to happiness and freedom. Without view, without a wise understanding of the cause of happiness, all you have is technique. Until you see your mind, your mate, and your relationship with clarity and realize that happiness lies within, you will keep trying to control the outer circumstances and change reality to make yourself feel better. That will have limited success. You've probably already discovered that typical couples' skills don't fix your relationship. They don't address the fundamental problem—wrong view. As long as you keep believing that it is your partner's job to make you happy, happiness will elude you. You must shift your view and rewrite your love story in order to create love and passion that lasts a lifetime.

We Are Story-Making Machines

Imagine you are driving to the grocery store and traffic is heavy. You see a little red car speeding up behind you. The driver weaves in and out of traffic, zooms by you with a loud honk, and runs the yellow light. What story do you make up about the driver, and how does that story affect you? Now, let's say the red car races by, but this time you notice a sign on the back as it flies through the yellow light. The sign says, "Children's Hospital Organ Donor Transport—Please Yield to Save a Child." What is your story this time, and how does this story make you feel?

We are story-making machines. All day long, we receive information, or data. We perceive it by filtering it through our own experiences, culture, preferences, and biases. And then we add idiosyncratic interpretations. In other words, we distort reality—the data itself—and create a story. Now, the story-making part is not the problem. The problem is that we then believe that our story is actually real. You believe that the driver of the red car is an inconsiderate jerk, or you believe she is a compassionate hero, based on which bits of data you have and how you interpret them.

Challenging the truth of your view is similar to evaluating the truth of a movie. A movie is simply the play of light and movement on a screen. Yet, it can feel very real—you can laugh, cry, feel anger, or get sexually aroused by the story. But if someone asked you, "Is this really happening?" you'd laugh and say, "No, it's just a movie." You would see the truth of the story—that it is simply a story—even though when the creepy clown jumped out of the closet, your fear sure felt real. Loving view is about developing the wisdom to recognize that your own mental movie is not reality, no matter how emotionally compelling it is. So how does this play out with your mate? Well, if you want to be happy in love, stop clinging to your story and insisting it is real. Start seeing that there are two sides to the story.

Last night I had a session with a couple, Jordan and Savannah, who'd just returned from a friend's wedding. Savannah had been anxious because Jordan's ex-girlfriend Jasmine would be at the wedding. So, she'd asked him to avoid Jasmine. At the wedding, Jordan ended up speaking with Jasmine and told his ex that he and Savannah were going for fertility treatment. Savannah overheard, left in tears, Jordan followed her, and they argued.

As they sat on my couch, I saw that there were two different stories, each based on partial data. My job was to help this couple see that too. Jordan's story was that when Jasmine told him she was engaged and pregnant, he'd told her how happy he was with Savannah and how they, too, were planning a family. He said, "I was kind of bragging about how great you are and how well we are doing. I thought you'd like that." Savannah's story was that her boyfriend had broken his promise to avoid his ex, and instead, he had shared vulnerable information about her pregnancy struggles with a woman she disliked. She felt betrayed by him, and her jealousy toward Jasmine was triggered.

One event, two stories. But the damage to this couple was significant because they each believed their own story to be true. From his side, Savanah is impossible to please and insecure for no reason; from her side, Jordan betrayed her trust. According to loving view, neither story is real. Each is a fabricated reality based on partial data. But because both people are clinging hard to their perception, they are unable to accept that their partner saw a different movie. Reality doesn't hurt, but the story in their mind sure does.

So, what's the solution? Well, according to the Buddha, we need to strip away our story and stop embellishing the facts. In other words, we need to see things as they really are: two people who love each other, two different views, and a choice to either cling to the story and suffer or let go and be happy.

MINDFUL SKILL: Seeing What Is— Mindfulness of Breathing

Meditation doesn't just belong on your cushion; it belongs in your love life. If you want to learn to see the data instead of believing your story, begin by practicing mindfulness of breath. The practice is to cultivate nonjudgmental awareness of what's actually happening without interpretation. Directly experience breathing in and breathing out. Then examine the stories you project on the breath. With practice, you will learn to see your partner under the stories you project on them.

Begin by settling into a meditation posture. Then let your mind roam and notice what you are experiencing—any thoughts, feelings, physical sensations, sounds, or other sense data. Try to just notice, without judgment. For example, if you notice your knee is a bit sore, try to simply accept the current data of "sore knee." Rather than disliking the soreness, deciding sore knees are bad, or making up a story about how your sore knee will ruin your golf game tomorrow, play with trying to just notice the data.

Next, slowly begin to focus your attention on the physical sensation of breathing in and breathing out. You may wish to place your attention on your belly, on your chest, or at the tip of your nostrils, using one of those three places to anchor your attention. Let's say you choose your belly. Really try to experience the physical sensation of your body breathing—the movement of your belly on the inhale and on the exhale. When your attention wanders and you start thinking about watering your garden or become distracted by the sound of a dripping tap, see if you can catch yourself making up a story. *I'll make a veggie curry for dinner* and *Maybe I can get that discount plumber to stop by* are just stories. They are not real, and they are not happening here and now. What is the data? Just the act of sitting still, attempting to pay attention to the breath. Can you practice letting go of the story and simply experiencing breathing? When you get trapped in a story, no problem. Just notice how easy it is to project something onto nothing, and then try to drop the story and return to the simple data of the sensations of the body breathing. Repeat, over and over. Keep turning off the movie projector. Get to know the screen. Practice letting go of believing the movie.

Visit http://www.drcherylfraser.com/buddhasbedroom for a guided meditation on mindfulness of breathing.

Not Wrong, Just Different

When you argue, each partner's story feels very real. So, you are at a stalemate. Yet, both stories are just opinions based on incomplete view. When you hang on to your view as the only view, the right view, you will suffer, and so will your sweetheart. The harder you hang on, the more emotional your defense of your story gets. You feel anxious and angry and cling even tighter, demanding that your sweetheart admit that you are right and they are wrong. But who's right, anyway? Your story is not right. It is your view, your preference, and your interpretation. Perception is not reality. It is not the way things really are—it is simply the way things are for you. And your partner's story is not wrong. It is just a different view, preference, and interpretation.

But stories can split you apart. I once worked with a couple who divorced over the dishwasher. He had a military background, and he liked the dishwasher to be loaded in a very specific, meticulous manner, the plates and cups as orderly as new recruits, standing at attention in precise order of height, weight, and eye color. He criticized his wife for the way she loaded the dishes and demanded that she learn his system and do it his way, the right way. While she made a half-hearted attempt to treat the flatware like toy soldiers, more often than not, she would toss the dishes in and press start. This enraged him. He clung to his story that he was right, she was wrong, and she had to see it that way. Try as I might, I could not get him to acknowledge that her way was okay too. He became more bitter and contemptuous and said if she wouldn't do it the right way, he would leave.

Was that loving view? Obviously not. He couldn't see that his partner was not wrong, just different. Rather than fight, he could have accepted her story and perhaps offered, with a smile, to do the dishes. But by hanging on so hard to his version of reality, he could not see the illusion of his own story. It was as though he was stuck inside an endless movie and did not know that he could get out simply by turning the projector off. He completely believed that his wife's behavior was the cause of his pain and that the only way to fix his pain was for her to do what he needed her to do. He wanted reality—and his wife—to fall in line and salute.

Maybe his reaction seems a little extreme to you. But is it completely unfamiliar? We do the same thing each time we disagree with our partner and get huffy about being right. We want to change their view, change our partner, and turn them into someone who sees things the way we do. Instead, can we make our view a loving one? Can we change how we look at our sweetheart, at the circumstances of the argument, at the data itself? An awakened lover is able to let go of their ego and the irrational need to be right.

LOVE SKILL: The Other Side of the Clock

Three days a week, I trot up the cement stairs that separate my home from my office. I take a moment to enjoy the ocean view—reminding myself that the ocean I see is only a fraction of the complexity of "ocean," that what I see is just my perspective. Then, I welcome the first couple of the day. Now imagine you and your mate are on the couch in my office. I'm across from you, and on the table next to me is a small clock. I pick up the clock. I turn to you, and I show you the front of the clock and ask you to describe what you see using any word except "clock." You reply, "I see a hand-sized object with eight sides. It is gold and has roman numerals." Then I turn to your partner and show them the back of the clock and ask them to describe what they see. Your sweetheart says, "It's a sort of square thing, it is black, and it has a kickstand and two round dials."

Now I ask the key question: "Who's right?" You say, "Well neither of us is right," or "We are both right." And yet you were looking intently at the same thing and trying to see it accurately. This exercise is a powerful reminder that you only ever see what you see—it is a partial view—and your partner's perspective may be very different. So how can you apply this to your relationship? Remember that when you are having a disagreement or misunderstanding, you are simply seeing different sides of the same thing. Instead of automatically defending your story, "It's gold with Roman numerals, not black with a handle!" remind yourself that the clock has more than one side and that your partner's story is valid too.

I invite you to take this idea into your life in the following way. When you bump up against your partner's view, instead of trying to force them to see things your way, ask them, "What do you see from your side, sweetheart? Because I can't see it. Help me understand." Then listen with loving view. Don't convince them they are wrong. Move out of conflict and into mindful loving.

Work on simply catching yourself wanting to prove that your story is right. Remember the clock. Remind yourself to let go of clinging and to get curious about the other side. Adopt loving view and love like a Buddha.

Would You Rather Be Happy or Right?

If you want to be happy, stop trying to change your partner's view. You can't. But then, you already know that, don't you? The only mind you need to change is yours—which is good because it is the only mind you have potential mastery over.

I met with a couple recently who recounted an argument that had almost ruined their anniversary weekend. They were driving to a ferry that would take them to a romantic island when they received a message asking them to bring extra drinking water as the well was running low. Letice jogged across the street for water and snacks while Sarah got gas. Sarah states, "I *told* her to buy the big water bottles. It was only at the ferry that I saw she bought four cases of tiny plastic water bottles! She *knows* I hate those things! We'd just had a friend who sails the world tell us about running into a massive plastic ball out in the ocean!" As she tells her story, Sarah becomes visibly agitated. There is anger and hurt in her demeanor, and her voice is cold and strident. Letice looks weary as she tells me, "The small bottles were way more economical. She's been worrying about finances, and I wanted to save us some money. But she freaked out on me for trying to do the right thing. Then we were both mad, and we didn't talk all the way to the cabin." So much for the romantic weekend. Or can it be salvaged?

The sad thing about this familiar story is that both people suffer. The need to be right, and the unwillingness to try to understand the alternate reality of the beloved, hurts. When we hold on to our view in opposition to another, it's all because we want to be "right."

What's the desperate need to be right all about, anyway? You can blame evolution for it. We are hardwired to respond to the world by trying to protect ourselves. At a deep level, our ego is running around saying, "What's in it for me? I need to be happy and safe! Me first!" In Buddhism, this self-referencing ego is seen to be the cause of all of our suffering. Our personal reality is an autobiographical movie starring "ME!" as the hero fighting desperately against the bad thing with big teeth that wants to hurt us, take our stuff from us, or kill us. Sure, we don't consciously think our mate is a saber-toothed tiger, but when they have a different view from us—they value penny-pinching over saving the planet, in Sarah's view—we automatically react to them as though they are an enemy. Our ego feels threatened, it struggles to feel safe, fight-or-flight chemicals flood our body, and we go on the attack. Metaphorically, we pick up our sharpened stick and fight our sweetie until they back down and say yes, you are right, honey, and I am wrong.

If you want to be happy in love, you need to learn to override your inner caveman and manifest your awakened lover. This is easy to say and difficult to practice, but mindfulness helps. When you slow down and take a closer look at your view—sort of like slowing down a piece of film and looking at the frames that make up the story on the screen—you can see through the illusion that seems so real. This is what Letice and Sarah did when they arrived at the cabin. They perched on the deck, held hands, and asked each other to explain their side of the clock, so to speak. Sarah's story was that Letice never listens to her and belittles her environmental activism. Letice said she knew Sarah was worried about how much the anniversary weekend cost, so she was trying to save money, and that she felt criticized for being thoughtful.

In order to be happy, this couple simply needed to view the facts differently—to view the situation through a lens of mindful loving, not self-preservation, and to choose happy over right. So next time you find yourself arguing with your sweetheart, be mindful. Realize you are in fact arguing with your own mind. You can be right, and protect your ego, or you can be happy, and love this imperfect person who sometimes sees a very different movie than you. Once you can really understand that, you can let go of expectations and create space between the two views in which understanding and love can bloom again.

MINDFUL SKILL: Identifying the Expectations Behind the Unhappiness

Since cave-boy first met cave-girl, partners have been trying to change each other. *If only* they liked tango dancing, or initiated sex more, or took me to Tahiti … So much relationship misery is caused by our attempts to get what we want. But beware of the insidious *if only.* This thinking points to the fatal flaw in the scramble to live a pain-free life. It has an inherent assumption that sets you up for suffering—*if only* the one I love would change, *then* I would be happy.

I encourage you to develop a daily mindfulness practice of identifying expectations and catching the insidious *if only* … This will help you build the muscles needed for letting go. In meditation, we practice paying attention to what is. We also practice, over and over again, letting go of expectations. We practice letting go of wanting the experience to be different. Try this in your relationship. Using mindful awareness, identify your expectations when they pop up and see them for the trap they are. When you are unhappy with your mate, can you identify the unmet expectation? The subtle *if only?* Ask yourself, What did I expect, and what did I get instead? Then notice how that unmet expectation is what is making you miserable. It isn't actually your mate that is causing the pain—it is your mind. Loving view sees this. Practice accepting your mate, and yourself, just as you are. Because under the cloud of *if only*, this moment is beautiful and perfect, and pain free, just as it is.

Kill the Soulmate and Save Your Relationship

Shaun Cassidy, teen singing idol and one of TV's sexy Hardy Boys, was my soulmate. There I was clad in the kilt and knee socks of a private school girl, lusting over this blue-eyed heartthrob and completely convinced we would fall in love. Turns out Shaun was not my soulmate. I look back at the confused girl I was with a mixture of amusement and compassion. I was suffering. I thought my perfect mate existed. Perhaps you did, too. Back then many of us believed if we could only find that one special person, he or she would make us happy, ever after. So, how's that working out?

The problem is that now I'm in my fifties, not my teens, and yet traces of that longing can still invade my mind and bedevil my relationship. I love my sweetheart, but he is definitely not my soulmate either. He isn't perfect, and he doesn't make me happy all the time. And I'll admit that sometimes I freak out and become convinced that I have committed to the wrong person, that my "real" partner is still out there. That guy writes books on neuro-cognition, creates nonprofits to adopt street dogs, and is a tantric master. Deep down I still carry a subconscious soulmate template, which is updated frequently as my own interests and values evolve. And when I am not paying attention, my mind compares the imperfect human I spend my life with—who is currently snoring in the bedroom while I write—to the ideal hunk in my head.

Funny? Perhaps. Our minds are fairly ridiculous. We so easily fall into confused view, forgetting the facts of life and clinging to wanting something else, something better. But it's a lot less funny if we indulge these thoughts, inviting them to hijack the present moment and sweep us into the emotionally booby-trapped land of *what if*. What if I leave my partner and seek the man who is *really* meant for me? Well, here is what I would find if I looked: not someone better, but someone different. New guy would have some qualities my partner lacks and lack some of the qualities my partner has. The suffering part of this is the unexamined, incorrect assumption that new guy would be perfect. He'd make me happy all the time. But the four facts of life clearly teach that is not the case.

We all chose the wrong person—if we expect that person to make us happy all the time. When we look at our sweetheart through the lens of a soulmate template, we will see all the places they don't fit our fantasy. When we focus on the parts that don't fit, we are miserable. It is our incorrect view that's the problem, not our sweetheart. This soulmate trap is subconscious and powerful. Like a shark, it lurks, waiting for a moment of disgruntlement with your current relationship and takes a bite out of your contentment. Using mindful awareness, identify your unrealistic expectations when they pop up and see them for the trap they are. Then carefully sidestep the trap and step into loving view. Wipe the lens clean of your soulmate taint, and you can begin to see the one you love clearly—snoring and all.

The longing for the illusory perfect soulmate pretty much dooms your current relationship. No human can live up to the picture you have in your head. You will always be dissatisfied until you show up here and now with mindfulness. Loving view means seeing reality as it is, without expectations. So stop looking for perfection and be happy with the imperfect mate you already have. Embrace what is, instead of longing for what is not, and you can rest in the love that is always present. Wrong view is a cloud over the sun. Under the cloud, passion and connection are always shining. Dissolve the wrong view, and you can fall in love all over again with the one you are already with. That's how the thrill can last forever.

LOVE SKILL: Focus on What Is Present, Not What Is Missing

You've seen how this soulmate template can really mess up your relationship. So, you need to kill the soulmate. At the end of chapter 3, you created your lover list—your own personal top ten qualities you want in your relationship. I invite you to review your list and update it if your priorities have changed. Then consider this. Your mate is not a ten—they don't have all of the things you want. Because the ten-out-of-ten mate doesn't exist—that is the mythical soulmate. Most couples I speak to in my private practice, or coach in my online programs, report that their mate has about seven of the ten qualities they want in a partner. How about you? How many of your lover list qualities does your sweetheart demonstrate, at least part of the time? If you want to be happy in love—and I know you do—look carefully for the qualities your partner has, instead of the ones they lack. The cause of your longing, your discontent, your "if only" is focusing on what you don't have, instead of what you do.

So first, compare your mate to your lover list. Next, explore your own view. Do you tend to focus on the missing qualities (your partner doesn't like to travel) or the qualities that are present (your partner has great integrity, a dazzling sense of humor, and is very patient with your kids)? Then make a commitment to deliberately pay attention to what is present, instead of focusing on what is missing. Move away from wanting and into letting go. See your beautiful mate as they really are. In this way, you can be 100 percent happy with seven out of ten.

Love Bytes

💜 Your partner is not wrong, just different. Practice accepting them as they are.

💜 When you argue with your mate, you are arguing with your own mind.

💜 An awakened lover can rewrite the story and choose to be happy instead of right.

💜 Kill the soulmate to save your relationship—focus on the good, not what's missing, and love the one you're with.

Buddha Bytes

🪷 If you want to uncover the thrill, don't change who you are looking at; change how you are looking. That's loving view.

🪷 We are story-making machines—but don't be fooled; the story isn't real. Wisdom sees things as they really are.

🪷 In meditation, you cultivate nonjudgmental awareness of what is happening. In love, do the same: see your beloved without judgment.

🪷 Beware of if only. Expectations interfere with love. Let go of wanting and sink into the happiness underneath.

CHAPTER 5

Loving Intention

Falling in Love Is Easy,
But Staying in Love
Takes Mindfulness

When you woke up this morning, felt your partner's foot warm against your calf, and opened your eyes to the sight of their tousled hair, did your feel a rush of thrill? If you are like most people in a long-term relationship, you probably slid out of bed and turned on the shower instead of turning toward your beloved with curiosity and delight. But what if this was the first time that beautiful person spent the night? Ah yes, then your interest and actions this morning would have been different.

What changed to make the thrill decline? Arguably not your partner's inherent desirability. It is your view toward having this person in your early morning sheets that has shifted. You are used to them. Your love affair is no longer new. Novelty is thrilling, and familiarity is not. You have changed how you think about your lover and how you react to your relationship.

So, does that mean the thrill is gone forever? Certainly not. Thrill is always there under the clouds of complacency. To find it, you need to set loving intentions—to vow to make your love affair new, interesting, and fun once again. This is how you become passion. Remember, great passion doesn't just fall out of a tree and bonk you on the head. Awakened lovers decide to see their beloved with fresh eyes by reminding themselves to seek out and magnify their partner's positive traits and minimize the negative ones. They deliberately set out to cherish their mate, to surprise them, and to be surprised. Thrill is an intentional stance. Do you want to love like a Buddha? First, change your view. Next, identify the clouds of familiarity and choose to penetrate them. Deliberately cultivate novelty. Contact the shining wonder and romance of this moment with this person right here and now, with mindful attention.

Fall in Love Again with the One You Are With

Falling in love is easy. You chase those glorious falling-in-love feelings as hard as you can, and when you catch them, you clamp down like your life depends on it. You have excitement, focus, and interest—the ingredients of thrill. You develop intimacy as you share your history, hopes, and dreams. You pursue sensuality with presence and delight, intentionally choosing seductive underwear and planning an evening that will dazzle your date. Passion blooms without effort, a perfect triangle of thrill, intimacy, and sensuality resting on a bed of novelty.

Novelty is thrilling. That's why it's so easy to fall in love. But your initial passion rests on a shaky and impermanent foundation— by definition, new cannot last. Routine, safety, and predictability— the foundation of a stable, committed relationship—can feel ho-hum. And ho-hum is not good for thrill. Routine is the antithesis of surprise. If your partner strides in the door, kisses you passionately, and hands you a fistful of fresh picked poppies, you are delighted. Your heart jumps, and you feel like the luckiest person in the world. Now, imagine that your partner greets you that way every day for fourteen years. Does your heart still jump each time? Probably not. If you are not mindful, once the novelty wears off, you get bored with the same old plaything. You may stop doing what used to come easily—planning romantic weekends, listening with open nonjudgmental curiosity to your sweetie, wearing black lace instead of saggy cotton. The new becomes familiar, the surprising becomes routine, and you develop lazy love habits. Marriage Inc. replaces Dating Inc. You stop paying attention to your lover and your love relationship. The thrill fades away, your former passion neglected like a forgotten squirrel in the dog toy basket.

Wouldn't it be fantastic if you could go back to the beginning and find each other new again? Well, you can. To break complacent habit patterns, to move out of Marriage Inc. and into becoming passion, you must *make love intentional*. After the initial throes of falling in love, you cannot rely on lust and novelty to keep you interested. You must nurture thrill with loving intention. And there are two main ways you can do that. First, by intentionally developing mindfulness—noticing, appreciating, and connecting with the present moment and with your lover in this present moment. When you pay deep attention, you can create novelty over and over again with the one you are with and replace boredom with fascination. Second, by setting intentions to bring the thrill back by planning romance, bringing creativity to your sex life, and generally kicking routine in the butt. Decide to bring your sweetheart poppies. Or surprise them with something new. And when you receive poppies, be mindful that poppies, and your sweetheart, are inherently beautiful whether this is the first time you have ever seen them or the hundredth. For believe it or not, every moment together is new and exciting if you simply set your mind to it.

MINDFUL SKILL: Bust Love Boredom by Getting Interested

For every fascinating man or woman, there can be a partner who finds them boring after all these years. Remember, a bored mind has simply ceased to be interested. Your own mind of curiosity may need a jump-start. Set aside a time to sit with your partner and ask each other interesting questions. This is a fantastic way to remain curious and to discover new things about the person you may have slept beside every night for decades. You can do this at home, but better yet, do it out at a funky bistro or on a park bench, creating novelty with the setting as well as the questions. The questions should be open-ended and encourage lengthy replies. They can be playful or serious, simple or deep. In this present moment, you can create curiosity by opening your eyes and heart and seeing this amazing human in front of you with a fresh mind. Now, if you're not the world's most creative person and it's difficult for you to think of questions, I'll get you started with some ideas—questions to inspire intimacy, thrill, and sensuality, and some just for fun. But it's the quality of curiosity you bring to the enterprise, more than the questions themselves, that matters. So, for the next month, set the intention that once a week you will ask each other five meaningful questions. Then sit back and see what happens.

- ❧ If you won a contest that gave you four vacation houses anywhere in the world, what four places would you choose, and why?

- ❧ How did you meet your first best friend, and what happened to that friendship?

- ❧ Most of us secretly fear that the world will see through us and into our biggest weaknesses and vulnerabilities. What parts of you do you never want the world to know about?

- ❧ What is the most public place you've ever made love? Who was it with?

- ❧ If you could trade lives with another person for one day, who would you pick and what would you do?

- I know I'm not perfect, and neither are you, my love. If you had a magic wand and could abolish one annoying habit from each of us, what would you get rid of?

- What is something you have always wanted to try—a sport, a trip, a business venture—but fear or doubt stopped you?

- If you could go back in time and spend ten minutes with yourself when you were twenty-one years old, what would you say?

- When it comes to our sexual life, what is one thing you wish we would do more often or try for the first time?

- What album, singer, or band had the biggest impact on you in your teens, and why?

Intend to Create Novelty

How good are you at creating novelty and interest? Are you doing it intentionally? If not, is it happening on its own? Let's take today as an example. Have you taken a moment to study the face you know so well and feel love and gratitude? Did you choose to learn something new about your sweetie over breakfast—maybe by asking them to tell you about the best breakfast they ever ate? (Mine involved spoon-standing-straight-up melty hot chocolate, glistening croissants, and the bird-laden trees of the Italian countryside.) Did you tease them into a quickie in the shower or at the very least kiss them good-bye—with tongue? You may be one of the rare couples who master keeping passion and thrill alive. If so, keep it up. More likely, you need to intentionally uncover and cultivate passion once again. Don't worry, you can. Choose to deliberately create what happened easily in the beginning. Intend to create novelty.

A few couples are great at maintaining thrill, and I see them as an inspiration. For example, last week I dropped in to my local computer shop and was delighted to see an old friend. She and I used to ride horses together as kids—when ponies were still way more interesting than cowboys. She's now married to the hunk she dated in high school. They live in a romantic lakeside heritage farmhouse where she teaches horseback riding full time. Now, here is the thrill part of the story. While we were comparing notes on life and love, she hands her smartphone to the computer tech. A second later, her text alert pings. The techie glances at the screen and asks with a grin—he knows my friend and her hubby—"Who is ICE?" "Oh," she replies, "that's Brent; he's my In Case of Emergency." The tech proceeds to read the text out loud. My friend blushes the chestnut shade of my childhood pony Rusty. Her husband of twenty-four years had texted her randomly in the middle of an ordinary Tuesday these four words: "What are you wearing?"

Now that's what I'm talking about. Be mindful. Set loving intention and plan to keep the thrill alive. Then act on those intentions. Make an effort. In the beginning, it was easy to send spontaneous sexy messages to the person you were infatuated with. These days, it takes intention. Passion is a choice, not an accident.

LOVE SKILL: Plan for Novelty

The thrill can last forever; it just needs a little help. One way to do that is by planning dates that spark curiosity and create a sense of adventure. When you are doing something exciting— perhaps zip lining off a mountain—you find your partner more attractive. Your adrenaline is flowing, and that helps mimic novelty and thrill. Sure, your partner may not be new, but zip lining with them is a new experience.

Brainstorm some fun, out-of-the-box ideas and commit to a monthly novelty date. Here are a few ideas for a "not your typical date night" to get you started.

- ♥ Plan something new and adventurous—a tango lesson, a visit to a theme park, horseback riding, rock climbing, an erotic massage class, a midnight ghost tour in a haunted city.

- ♥ Recreate your very first date in as much detail as you can. But during this "second first date," tell your partner what you were thinking and feeling when you met them.

- ♥ Plan something erotic (but something you do not normally do)—take a class in sensual massage, go to a sexy costume ball, visit a love shop and buy a toy or game (and then use it).

Love Boredom and Affairs

Love boredom runs rampant in many long-term relationships—both outside and inside the bedroom. As your love affair transitioned from new and exciting to familiar and pleasant, you lost that loving feeling. And here you are, with a severe case of love boredom. Your spouse used to be so interesting. And then they got boring.

Except they didn't. Your mate is never boring. Your head is. You have a bored mind. And while you may not be able to change your partner, you can definitely change your own mind. Perhaps you need to make more effort to see your beloved as the cool creature they are. Maybe you feel bored because you have a mind that is not seeking to experience your sweetie with open awareness—the way you did when you were falling in love with them. Maybe you think you know your spouse so well that you actually believe there is nothing left to learn about them. Think about that for a moment. Do you really believe this complex beautiful person has no more layers for you to explore?

You and your spouse are both fascinating people who may have forgotten to treat each other that way. You've gotten complacent. And complacency can lead to affairs. When you, or your spouse, feel taken for granted, you are much more susceptible to the attention of another. When someone new treats you, or your spouse, like the special person you are, intrigue and attraction can flourish. And those "falling in love" hormones and brain chemicals, the ones churned out by novelty, start hopping. It is easy to mistake this temporary false intimacy for the real thing and to mistake lust for love. If you are not mindful of these processes playing out, you may end up in bed with a stranger. The path from boredom to betrayal can be shorter than you'd think.

Once an affair happens, the relationship ends, right? Actually, research indicates that more than half of couples survive the betrayal of an affair—that is, they do not break up. This finding surprises most people. But it doesn't surprise me. An affair wakes the couple up. It shakes them into seeing each other anew. "If that person found my spouse desirable, maybe they still are." "I betrayed the person I love because I was bored, and I almost lost them. I vow to cherish my partner from now on." The couple that moves through a successful affair-recovery period ideally builds a new union, a more mindful, attentive, romantic, and spontaneous one.

Affairs certainly shatter boredom. But an affair is an extraordinarily painful way to wake up and begin to see your partner clearly. So instead of chasing novelty, learn how to bring novelty home. Make the effort to find your spouse fascinating again, to discover new things about their body and mind. If complacency and lack of imagination zapped excitement, you can bring it back. You can discover the riches of the present moment. You can see your beloved with fresh eyes and touch them as though it were the first time, by getting your head in the game. You can fall in love all over again with your sweetie, instead of looking for someone new. Have an affair with your mate. Because when you show up in this very moment, thrill is here and now, with the one you are already with.

The Thrill Can Last Forever—
Just Get Mindful

Imagine sitting on your meditation cushion, at one with your breath. You feel good—mindfulness is working. Right here, right now, there is nothing more interesting than this very moment. Suddenly you hear a voice you know so well, asking for the hundredth time, "Honey, have you seen my keys?" You now spend your meditation time wondering was this man, who counts picking up the car from the mechanic as a date, or this woman, who forgets to feed the cat but knows the plot of every reality TV show, *really* once the most fascinating person in the world?

The answer is yes. And they are still fascinating. You just forgot to be interested. It's up to you to awaken intimate emotional communion and sensual physical connection—and some mindfulness can give you the tools. How did you connect when you were still crazy about your sweetie? You paid close attention, you wanted to learn everything about them, and you tried not to judge. And let's face it, you couldn't wait to touch them. You were naturally focused and aware. To cultivate passion over the long term, you need to bring an open, loving, curious mind to your beloved as well as to your breath.

When you meditate or practice being mindful in daily life—as you drive, as you eat lunch—you train in paying attention to what is actually happening. You investigate this one breath without comparing it to every other breath you've had. You vow to be curious about whatever is happening, whether it is difficult or easy, unpleasant or pleasant. You attempt to be nonjudgmental—whether the mind is happy, sad, bored, or interested, you accept the moment and show up for it. Attention and curiosity don't just belong on your cushion. They belong in your life, in your relationship, and in your bed.

Thrill is a present-moment phenomenon. If you can connect deeply with this moment, you can experience it as it really is: a new, interesting moment, with a new, interesting partner. Think of it this way. If you love chocolate truffles and I hand you an exquisite Belgian confection, is there a bit of thrill? Yes. As you prepare to nibble this delicacy, your mouth waters. Ideally, you slow down and really experience the taste, the texture, the wonderful experience of melting goodness on your tongue. This truffle is interesting, appreciated, and sensual. Simply because you show up and deeply experience this truffle right now. Even though you have consumed hundreds of chocolates before. Now, apply that level of appreciation to your sweetheart. Let's say you sit down tonight at the end of a long day, and your beloved starts to share the details of the sales meeting with corporate headquarters. You hear about these meetings every week. Do you find the conversation delicious? Just like the hundredth truffle? You can, if you put your mind to it. Pretend this is a first date and you are attempting to learn who this person is. Pay attention to the nuances of your partner's voice and body language. See if you can learn what fires your sweetie up, what frustrates them, and if they have creative ideas about how sales can be improved. Remind yourself how multifaceted this person—the person you love but may take for granted—is. Whether or not you find sales meetings inherently interesting, your sweetie is interesting. Certainly, they are far more interesting than a single breath. Just like when you meditate, when you listen to your beloved, you can be mindful and practice noticing what is, with curiosity. Show up and connect with them instead of checking out.

So, the thrill can last forever, and Buddha-mind is key. When you become present, you can become passion. Everything old is new again if you bring a mind of newness to it. For example, when you are on the couch and you hear your spouse rattling their keys at the door, do you jump up to hug and kiss them? If not, take a lesson in thrill from your dog. Rover treats every homecoming like it was the first-ever homecoming—jumping, wagging, and showering the beloved with love and excitement. You, too, can make every hello the best hello. Moment-to-moment mindfulness—which you practice on your cushion—can help you do that. Because whether you are with her in a Darjeeling tea shop on your honeymoon or sharing a steaming cup over the wooden table he made for your twentieth anniversary, this moment, this warmth in the palm, these eyes looking into yours are absolutely new. If only you have the mindfulness to see.

MINDFUL SKILL: Touch Your Partner with Deep Presence

Touching the one you love used to be thrilling. But even pleasurable erotic touch can seem so familiar that it becomes ho-hum. It's time to make touch thrilling again. This mindfulness practice builds on the mindfulness of body sensations exercise you learned in chapter 1. The difference is that here you will bring your focused attention to the sensation of touching your partner's body, rather than the sensations in your own body.

Sit with your partner in a quiet place where you won't be interrupted. For this exercise, keep your clothes on. (In the sensuality chapters, things will get naked, but it is helpful to start simply and build up your awakened lover touching with the basics.)

To begin, close your eyes. Spend a few moments settling into the body sensations of sitting, the sensations of the body breathing. Allow your attention to settle a bit, perhaps to slow down if the mind is willing to. If the mind is busy, just accept that, and bring the forefront of your focus to body sensations, to breath sensations. There is nowhere to go, nothing to do, but to be here side by side with your beloved, breathing.

Next, I invite you to gently take your partner's hand and lay it in your lap. With eyes closed, slowly begin to trace the outline of their hand with your fingertip. Move slowly. Attempt to bring focused attention to the touch sensations at your fingertip. Do you experience warmth? Cool? What is the feeling, the texture, of the skin? Notice any changes from smooth to rough, soft to firm. Your partner can focus on the sensations of being touched on their hand, their inner wrist. Which touch feels the most pleasant? What areas are sensitive; what areas less so? Focus deeply on every sensation. How much nuance can you experience?

After some time, stop moving your finger and simply rest it, touching your partner's hand or arm. Then meditate together for a few minutes, taking the point of touch contact as the meditation object. When the mind wanders, bring the attention back to that point of contact. Really experience touch. For this touch, right here and now, is absolutely new.

When you are ready, open your eyes. Smile at your sweetheart. And hug with presence.

Passion Is a Choice

The first step to creating an intentional relationship is to get clarity on what you really want—or rather, what your larger, wiser self wants. Ask the awakened lover part of you—the one with loving view, the one who sees that reality won't always meet your expectations and that your soulmate doesn't exist—what it wants in this relationship. I'll bet that wise part wants to move away from the suffering caused by wrong view and hanging on, and to move toward peace, love, and passion. Here are three steps you can take to make that happen.

First, *identify your relationship goals.* One way to do this is to review your lover lists. You can turn these desires into reality with loving intention. Remember, intentions bridge your desire to visit Paris with the actions that will deliver you to Paris. Without intention, all you have are daydreams. You can dream about passion all you want, or you can intend to uncover and manifest it.

Once you have reviewed your love goals, the next step is to *set loving intentions*: specific, actionable aspirations that will help you create the awakened love you want. For example, let's say you put kindness and affection on your lover list. Applying that to your own relationship, say you decide you'd like to be more verbally affectionate toward your partner. Make that desire into a clear, actionable intention. Perhaps your loving intention is "I intend to say something sweet and romantic before I leave for work every morning." Or maybe you listed an exciting sex life as something you value. You might set the intention "I will plan a spicy seduction, something novel and exciting, once a month." Take some time to set some loving intentions.

Once you have set some intentions, you need to *take them into action*. I suggest you review your intentions frequently, schedule them into your calendar, and develop the habit of acting upon them. At first your old, lazy love habits will be stronger than your new intentions, so you will need to give yourself reminders. Put a sticky note on the doorknob that cues you to say, "I love you, wild thing," before you zip off to kickboxing class. Send your mate an invitation to a sensual date: "Sunday, 2:00 p.m., bedroom. Dress sexy, and I'll provide the handcuffs." Walk the bridge between desire and action. Become passion. Once you repeat the intended action over and over, it will gradually become a new habit. And perhaps you will text your sweetie, "What are you wearing?" on a regular basis—one little intentional gesture to keep the thrill alive.

Remember, with mindful loving, the thrill can last forever. It just needs a little help. Once you realize that, reviving romance is actually possible. It involves paying attention, acting in loving ways, creating novelty, and setting loving intentions.

LOVE SKILL: Set Wise and Loving Intentions

Loving intentions guide your behavior in the present moment and help you create an intentional relationship.

Step 1: Pick a relationship goal.

Goal: *I want to have more kindness in our relationship.*

Step 2: Choose several intentions that will guide you to act in ways that will move you toward that goal.

Intention 1: *I intend to speak with a kind tone when I feel impatient.*

Intention 2: *I intend to leave a meaningful and loving note for my spouse each morning.*

Intention 3: *I intend to meditate for thirty minutes most days to continue to strengthen my mind and cultivate patience.*

Step 3: Create your loving intentions list and then commit to spending two minutes each morning reviewing that list and setting your intentions for the day. Choose one or two to focus on. Then, commit to spending two minutes at the end of the day reviewing your progress. How did you do? Did you turn your intentions into actions? Some wins, some losses? Can you tweak your intentions to make them even more actionable? Your list is like a map, and if you use it well, it will help guide you to where you want to go. After a week of intentional practice, you should begin to experience how this exercise can help you make tangible movement toward your relationship goals. You may then wish to incorporate this practice as an ongoing awakened lover skill.

You can watch a video where I speak further about the loving intention practice at http://www.drcherylfraser.com/buddhas bedroom

Love Bytes

♥ Novelty is thrilling. True passion happens when you create the new within the familiar. Instead of chasing novelty, bring novelty home.

♥ Your mate is never boring. Your mind is. Get interested, bust love boredom, and fall in love all over again.

♥ Dating actually took a lot of planning. Can you learn to date your mate again?

♥ Passion is a choice, not an accident. Love is an intentional stance.

Buddha Bytes

❀ Thrill is a present-moment phenomenon. And every moment is new, if you meet it with curiosity.

❀ It doesn't take a miracle to see your partner the way you used to—it just takes mindfulness. Awakened lovers see their partner with fresh eyes.

❀ Set love goals; intend to create novelty, connection, and passion. Then turn loving intention into action.

❀ Touch with deep presence and awaken the sensuality of this moment.

PART III

INTIMACY

THE MINDFUL
LOVING PATH

CHAPTER 6

Loving Action
Demons and Antidotes—
Think Before You Act

Awakened lovers are intimacy ninjas. As you recall, I define intimacy as a deep emotional connection created by shared experiences, vulnerabilities, and acceptance. Intimacy—or what researcher John Gottman calls *marital friendship*—is a strong predictor of long-term marital happiness. So, I place it at the base of the passion triangle. Intimacy is what keeps us in an imperfect romantic relationship with our "definitely not my soulmate" over the long haul. Intimacy is the glue that holds our love boat together when it goes over painful and bumpy rapids, when love boredom zaps thrill and dampens the sizzle of sensuality. But the reliable old intimacy boat needs maintenance too. Even the greatest love affairs can go the way of the *Titanic* if the captains don't pay attention to intimacy.

"I just feel so alone—like I don't know you anymore," says Steven. His voice cracks as he looks pleadingly at his wife Joleen. I watch her carefully, wondering how she will respond to his longing. Joleen sits, immobile, with an annoyed look on her face. "What do you mean? We spend more time together than we used to—how can you possibly feel lonely?" What Steven is trying to explain is that in spite of the lush vacations and Sunday sex, he feels a terrible sense of disconnect from Joleen. Yes, they "do" many things together. But from Steven's perspective, they do them side by side, with little emotional connection. Sadly, this marriage has intimacy impairment.

Steven used to feel as though Joleen had his back. They met when she was a medical resident and he was starting his organic food business. They fell in love hard and fast and married within a year. Back then, Steven felt deeply connected to Joleen. When they came together at the end of a grueling workday, they shared their work stress, recounted funny stories, and talked about their dreams for the future. "I could count on her to listen to my struggles and cheer me on. And I knew about her most heartbreaking patients and how she was feeling about her friendships. Now? It's like she's a stranger. I don't think we've had a meaningful conversation in months."

Maybe Steven and Joleen's story sounds familiar to you. After all, Marriage Inc. can leave you feeling like there is no time or energy to connect on a deep emotional level. So how can you create more intimacy? With action. The Buddha didn't teach us to simply sit in a cave meditating, changing our view, and setting intentions in our head. He taught us to act with wisdom and compassion. The next three steps of the mindful loving path—loving action, speech, and livelihood—are the prescription for how to behave like a Buddha in your quest to deepen your relationship intimacy and become passion.

A loving action is one that reduces suffering and increases intimacy. And a loving action originates with a loving mind state. So even though this chapter is about action, you will learn to work with the thoughts behind your actions. The Buddha was clear that the motivation or intention behind the action determines whether an action is loving and wholesome or not. Because intimacy and vulnerability are scary, even when you want to act kindly, you may fail—sometimes your psychological defenses make you act in ways that are not loving. Once you can recognize your fears and see how they corrupt your best intentions, you will be able to apply the antidotes, calm your mind, and act from your deeper, more awakened lover. Essentially, you need to think before you act so love can shine.

Intimacy Is Not for Wimps

If you love someone, trust someone, and let them inside your walls, you will get hurt. Dharma is about seeing things as they are. The truth of change means hurts will happen because you cannot hold onto anything forever—not a person, not a feeling, not even this very moment. This is the intimacy dilemma: Do you stay safe and disconnected from the one you love, or risk deep intimacy and the hurts that go along with it? Well, if you want great passion, you need deep intimacy. You must be willing to expose your vulnerabilities and to accept what happens next.

Intimacy takes fearlessness. In a moment of deep intimacy, you let down your guard and show your naked heart. You calm the stories in your head and see that this person cannot rescue you—but they can love you and hold your hand in the midst of this impermanent, unpredictable, and sometimes painful life. To really show up with your lover in this moment with naked presence takes a huge amount of courage. It means you choose to open up and be unprotected in the midst of impermanence. Can you act from love even when you are afraid? Can you say, "I love you," and choose to trust the partner who betrayed you? If you want awakened love and sustainable passion, you must feel the fear and do it anyway.

But first, you must clearly identify your fears. When I teach relationship intensives, I instruct the couples to take their fear of intimacy out of their head and into form. I ask them to create and display their most selfish, insecure, and nasty defenses—the fears that interfere with loving action. At a recent couples weekend, a svelte gorgeous woman held aloft her clay sculpture, a half-girl, half-dragon form. In the creature's chest was a sparkling pink jewel surrounded by bristling black spikes. She snarled, "This is my love demon. If you try to come near my heart, I will impale you on the spikes of my icy indifference." I pointed out that her scary doll shows glimpses of a tender heart, glowing and beautiful. "Aha!" she cried. "But if I let you near it, you might hurt me one day!" The group cheered her on. One by one, the students displayed their fears of intimacy. While each love demon is unique, they all share one theme: "I am afraid to get hurt." Now, you might wonder why we cheer something that stops us from being an awakened lover. We cheer because we recognize that our defenses don't mean to hurt us. Our defenses are actually trying to keep us safe. Letting go into love is scary, and intimacy is not for wimps.

After we cheer the love demons for trying to keep us safe, each person vows to let the demons go and let love in. They dissolve their sculpture and scatter the pieces in the forest. And then we dance in celebration, in the freedom and vulnerability that comes with risking intimacy. Loving action begins in the mind and then is made manifest in behavior and speech. For an action to be loving, it must be motivated by wise thoughts rather than fearful, selfish ones. So, if you want to act with love, you need to spot the love demons and dissolve them, over and over again.

Spot the Love Demons

"I miss you so much. You get home, turn on the TV, but never ask me about my day. When we have sex it's because I beg for it—how do you think that makes me feel?" Steven is close to tears as he pleads for his wife to pay attention to him. Joleen stiffens, and I watch her frustration build. Her shoulders tighten, and her facial expression grows cold, tight, contemptuous. "Don't be pathetic," she snaps. And like the Pacific Northwest rainclouds outside my office window, their love demons engulf them.

Does this sound familiar to you? We are basically nice people. We love our sweetheart. We intend to act in a loving manner toward them. But we find ourselves, all too often, acting from insecurity, anger, or a need to control. You may not act like an awakened lover—even when you really, really want to. What hijacks your loving intentions? Why is loving action so darn difficult?

The Buddha is very clear that there are three roots to all negative, destructive thoughts and actions—three main ways we defend our heart. He calls them the roots of greed, aversion, and confusion. According to him, these three mind demons cause all of our suffering. Remember, suffering is not defined as simply feeling sad or unpleasant—it is defined as what happens when we cling to wanting what we want, reject what we don't want, and try to control circumstances that we cannot control—just like we do when we are trying to get our needs met in our relationship. These three love demons are the big enemies of intimacy and loving action. When you are fighting to keep yourself safe and happy, your mate's happiness is forgotten, and your relationship is in trouble. But the demons are just trying to protect you—even if their methods are destructive. Don't hate them. Spot them, understand them, and learn to dissolve them by applying their antidotes. For under the cloud of selfishness, anger, and control lies the sun of their opposites. When you uncover the light of generosity, kindness, and compassion, you will think and then act with love. Then intimacy can flourish. So, let's learn to spot the love demons, apply their antidotes, and then take loving action.

Selfish Demon

The first root cause of suffering is wanting something. Sometimes called greed, clinging, or attachment, this demon seeks something that is not present, reaching out with its sticky hands and hanging on to illusory comfort. It believes that if it can only get a cuddle, a compliment, a cruise to the Caribbean, it will be happy. And so, it fights to get what it wants. When it comes to love, the selfish demon often shows up as insecurity, complaining, and neediness. Steven is in the grips of his selfish demon when he begs Joleen to give him what he believes he needs—"Please be curious about me; please seduce me; please show me affection." When Steven is not in the grips of this unpleasant mind state, he is able to approach his wife with confidence and offer connection, instead of demanding it. He invites her to join him at their favorite Thai restaurant, they share a lingering meal and conversation, and they both feel close and fulfilled. But when the demon has him in its grasp, he is consumed by his own needs. He is stuck in believing that she has to make him feel good. The selfish demon is self-pitying and whiny. Its slogan might be "But what about *me?*"

Antidote: Generosity. The antidote to the selfish demon is generosity and unselfishness. Recognize that the person you love has needs too. Your partner doesn't exist simply to make you happy. Generosity calls on us to move from "What about me?" to "What about you?" I love how the Buddha defines generosity. He emphasizes that to be truly generous, you must both give and receive in equal measure. We think of generosity as an outflow—*I am generous to you*—but he emphasizes that unless *I am open to receive from you*, I am not being generous. This is a beautiful teaching in loving relationship. It feels great. Plus, it calms the selfish demon because true giving includes true getting. When I give my heart, time, and attention to you, my heart is open to receive in turn the gifts you have to offer, and we can create the intimacy and connection that comes from the loving act of generosity.

In the couples therapy with Steven and Joleen, I gave him generosity homework. I pointed out that while he is at heart a really nice guy, when his selfish demon takes over, he treats his wife like his love ATM—a being who exists solely to give him stuff he wants. He desperately presses buttons, trying to withdraw affection and validation. He temporarily forgets that she is a feeling, thinking person with her own needs. I challenged him to explore what happens if he turns his get into a give: When he wants a cuddle, offer Joleen a foot rub. When he wants her to ask how his meeting with the plumber went, inquire about that tricky surgery she had today. I asked him to set daily intentions to give generously of his time, attention, and love. Each time he feels the sting of clinging and wanting, I instruct him to recognize the pain of selfishness and to deliberately shift his focus from "What are you going to do to make me happy?" to "What can I do to make you happy?"

To be generous is to be unselfish. And in order to be unselfish, we have to let go of what we want. Ultimately, wanting hurts, and the more we want, the more we suffer. The Buddha uses the analogy of a hot coal. When you grab onto a hot coal, it burns your hand. It hurts. If you want to stop the hurting, you have to let go. Selfishness seeks solace by holding the coal tighter. It will just hurt more. And we cannot give from a clenched fist, only from an open palm. So, I asked Steven to open his palm and his heart and practice putting his wife first. Because if Joleen gives in to his selfish demands for attention, he knows he doesn't feel much better. The attention he craves from her will only fill him up when it is freely given. And she can only give freely when he stops demanding. True generosity leads to loving action, in both directions.

MINDFUL SKILL: A Meditation on Generosity

Settle into a comfortable position. You can practice this meditation sitting or lying down. Because it is a heart-opening practice, gently supporting and nurturing the body is helpful.

Begin the practice with eyes open. Gently scan the environment around you with a soft gaze. Notice the objects, the shapes, the colors. Allow your gaze to settle on something pleasant, something beautiful. Appreciate the beauty.

Then allow your eyes to close. Simply rest, breathing and being. There is nothing to do, nowhere to go. Allow a sense of spaciousness and peacefulness to gently seep into your mind and body.

Next, allow yourself to bring to mind your partner. Your beloved. The complex and lovely being that you have chosen to spend your life with. This person has at times treated you with vast generosity. They have given to you great gifts of time, of attention, of patience. They have held you when you cried and surprised you with a gingersnap cookie placed on your pillow. For the next part of this practice, explore receiving and appreciating their generosity. Recall some specific instances where your partner has been generous toward you. Imagine the sweetness and thoughtfulness that motivated them to do these kind acts for you. Remember how you felt when you received those gifts of generosity. Allow your heart to soften into receiving. Notice what it feels like.

Then, in your own time, move into a meditation on giving. Recall some specific instances where you gave to your partner from a truly open, loving heart. Allow yourself to experience what it feels like to have a generous heart. To give freely, without selfishness or fear. To give from your best self. Spend some time relaxing into your open heart. Simply breathe in and breathe out, allowing your heart to be unguarded. Imagine your heart filling with a warm, pink light. Experience the joy of the generous heart.

After resting into your heart for some time, bring your partner to mind once more. Imagine their heart glowing with a warm, pink light. Then imagine the light spilling out from your heart, spilling out from their heart, and mixing in the space in between you. Smile at your partner and send to them the following heart wish:

May my heart be open to receive your generosity with joy and ease.

May my heart be open to give to you without limits.

May generosity flow between us, without separation.

May we always be able to contact and share our generous hearts.

Relax into the feeling of generosity and openness. Then allow the visualization to fade away and simply breathe into, and out from, your warm, good heart. When you are ready, open your eyes.

Angry Demon

The second root cause of suffering is not wanting something. Sometimes called aversion, avoidance, or hatred, this demon rejects what it does not want and tries to block it out or push it away. It believes that it cannot tolerate what is present, and so it must destroy whatever is making it miserable. When it comes to love, the angry demon often shows up as criticism, nastiness, and saying no to romantic and sexual overtures. Joleen is in the grips of her angry demon when she rejects Steven with her words and body language. She feels aversion to his needs, denies his feelings, and pulls away from him. When she is not in the grasp of this unpleasant mind state, she is able to open herself to the man she loves. She can recognize his longing, give him a hug, and tell him that she misses him too. But when the demon takes over, she wants to run away from unhappiness and build a wall around her heart. The angry demon is cold and mean. Its slogan might be "I hate you—go away and leave me alone."

Antidote: Kindness. The antidote to the angry demon is kindness and patience. Meanness is insidious. If you are not careful, it creeps into your love affair on tiny angry demon feet. Joleen reports that she is so worn down by Steven's neediness that she feels instant irritation when he makes any request. I watch her play this out in my office not just with her husband but also with me. I make a suggestion; she rejects it. I offer a comforting word; she bats it away with a sneer. Her angry demon is on high alert. But inside the spikes, I can see her glowing, vulnerable heart. She's aching for intimate connection with Steven, even as her actions drive them further apart. Intimacy is based in trust and understanding, and it cannot thrive in a climate of criticism and contempt. If this marriage is to have a chance, Joleen needs to stop pushing Steven away. She can calm her meanness by applying the anger antidote: kindness. But before she can be kind, she needs to learn the difference between reacting and responding.

Perhaps the most important skill I teach couples is first do no harm. If you are caught in the angry demon, don't react. Stop. Do nothing. Your body is flooded, caught in what is called "diffuse physiological arousal"—a fight-or-flight reaction fed by stress hormones and your reptilian brain. It is critical that you soothe yourself so you can *respond* to your mate like a sane person rather than *reacting* from anger and pummeling your sweetheart with your defensive artillery. By calming your body and examining your thoughts, you can create a gap between stimulus and response. This gives you a chance to be kind instead of cruel. Because in that gap, you can exercise choice. You can ask, "In this moment, do I choose to act from wisdom or from fear?"

Kindness is a choice. Whether you act in a kind manner is completely up to you. Sure, you may be in the grips of the angry demon, and you may not feel kind inside. But you can always fake it. You have the ability to act kind even when you feel angry or hurt. You can pause, take some breaths, and decide to respond warmly even when you are thinking, *I married an idiot.* The beautiful thing is that by acting kind, you may eventually begin to feel kind. Instead of jacking up the sympathetic nervous system—the part that floods you—by rejecting your spouse and creating more separation and anxiety, acting kind will begin to activate the parasympathetic system, the calm-you-down-and-bring-you-back-to-reality system. So, by acting kind, you can begin to soften your defenses and open up to intimate connection.

So, I invited Joleen to try some techniques when she's in the grips of her angry demon and is about to be mean. First, I asked her to stop, to not act or speak from anger. This will allow her to create a gap, a safe space where she can calm herself and choose how to behave. In that space, she scans her body and begins to self-soothe her physical agitation. Next, she scans and evaluates her thoughts and tries to be more kind in her mind. Instead of judging Steven harshly and automatically rejecting his requests, she practices creating affection for his quirks. When and only when she feels confident that she can respond from kindness instead of react from anger, she chooses to be kind to her friend—to act from mindfulness, not mindlessness. Meanness sucks, manners matter, and we all need to learn to punctuate our relationship with mindful loving gaps. For in that gap, kindness and clarity can be uncovered. Once you are calmer, you can thank the angry demon for trying to keep you safe. And then you can choose to be kind instead of mean.

LOVE SKILL: How to Soothe Your Flooded Body

How do you know if you are flooded and are at risk of reacting from anger and behaving unkindly? Your body will be agitated. Your heart rate will be high—likely over one hundred beats per minute (you can take your pulse to see if you are flooded). You may feel tightness in your shoulder muscles or jaw, a roiling stomach, or other physical stress symptoms. Your emotions may be agitated—anxiety, anger, or hurt may dominate. Alternatively, you may feel an odd sense of calm and disconnect, a cold detachment. Your thoughts may feel stuck, often in a one-sided argument, and you urgently want to make your partner listen to you. All of these warning signs tell you that you are physiologically altered and are unable to respond rationally and fairly. The angry demon is spoiling for a fight. As soon as you feel signs of flooding, stop talking and take no action. Next, deliberately start to soothe your flooded body to help your fight-or-flight system calm down. Here are a few techniques for self-soothing.

If possible, close your eyes (unless you are driving or using sharp knives). Then take at least three deep, slow, deliberate breathes. On the inhale, breathe in through your nose. At the top of the inhale, sip in a bit more air through your lips, as though you are drinking air through a straw. Hold your breath for a count of three. Then exhale through your mouth in a blowing motion. At the end of the exhale, blow out a bit harder—this will empty more air from the lungs and effectively create the experience of a vacuum. This will make your next inhale deeper. Again, sip at the top of the inhale, hold for three beats, exhale through the mouth, blow a bit extra, and go into big inhale number three. After the third exhale, allow the breathing to return to its normal pace.

Next, try calming your body with a tense-and-release exercise. Start with your hands. Form tight fists and clench the muscles tight, tighter, tighter still … then release your fists. Then tighten your fists and arms and shoulders tight, tighter, tighter still … then release. Then your neck, shoulders, and face, then your belly and back and butt, then your legs, knees, and feet. It's not important what order you choose, but try to clench and release as many muscles and body parts as you can. Then finish up with a whole-body clench—ball your fists up, curl your toes, clench your butt, pull your shoulders up, squish your face like you are sucking the world's most sour lemon. Tight, tighter, tighter still … then release your whole body. Ahh. The relaxation under the tension. The sun under the clouds.

Other ways to calm your physiology include meditating, using a calming visualization, going for a brisk walk, doing some jumping jacks, patting the dog, or baking muffins. As you apply mindful loving to your own life and relationship, you will learn what works best for you. But to begin, make a commitment to practice various ways you can stop action and calm your body when you are flooded.

Controlling Demon

The third root cause of suffering is confusion. Sometimes called delusion, wrong view, or ignorance, this demon forgets that you cannot fight reality. It believes that if you micromanage the world and your partner, manipulating until you get the external circumstances just right, you can keep yourself constantly safe and happy. When it comes to love, the controlling demon often shows up as a demanding control freak, very judgmental, and picky. In this guise, it fights desperately to fix what it thinks is broken, always on a relationship-improvement campaign but never able to relax into the love that is already here. But it can also swing the other way and become a passive victim. Because the controlling demon is confused, it decides relationship happiness is impossible and makes no effort to connect at all. The controlling demon is alternately demanding or exhausted, fighting for change or completely lazy and complacent. Its slogan might be, "If only you would do it right, then I'll be happy!" or "Love is too hard. I give up."

Antidote: Compassion. The antidote to the controlling demon is compassion and acceptance. After all, trying to control your partner and your relationship to get exactly what you want doesn't work. Okay, fair enough. But we've all experienced the painful reality that understanding something and being able to act upon it are two very different things. Simply wanting to let go of control doesn't dissolve the pattern. There must be a missing link—something that melts the control freak and uncovers clarity, something that truly inspires us to take loving action not because we believe we should, but because we are truly moved to act from love. That missing link is compassion. When you feel compassion, loosening control and acting with love is natural, easy, and right.

This week Joleen brought an example to my couch. "He's threatened that I make three times more money than he does. But how dare he tell me how to spend my cash." She feels controlled by Steven. I asked her to describe specific actions that trigger her. "When I wear a new dress he rolls his eyes, and I know he's thinking I spend too much on clothes. I want to add a deck with a hot tub, and he says I'm spoiled and our house is fine the way it is." I then guided Joleen to slow down, stop speaking, and breathe into her body. I asked her what sensations she feels. "My chest is tight. I'm angry and exhausted." I then asked her what story goes along with this experience. "He's so cheap. Why can't he be happy that I am well paid for work I love? He ruins everything." As she speaks that last thought, she looks sheepish. She turns to Steven and with a weak smile, says, "Sorry babe—obviously you don't ruin everything. I just get so frustrated that you can't enjoy our wealth with me."

In this moment, there is a crack in the clouds, and a ray of compassion seeps through. As we explore, Steven says he feels guilty that his business is not thriving. "What kind of husband needs his wife to pay for their anniversary trip? Every time the bills arrive, I feel like a failure." Joleen leans forward, touches his hand, tears at the corners of her eyes. Before she speaks, I hold up a finger, asking her to pause in the experience. I want her to notice what compassion feels like— to feel the moment when she sees her beloved's pain and her heart naturally softens; to observe her judgmental thoughts quieting down; and most importantly, to notice that when she sees his suffering, her need to control the situation melts away. Because ultimately, she loves Steven, and she wants to help. We then agree that compassion feels much better than control.

Compassion is the desire to free our partner from their suffering. It has three aspects. First, you must recognize that your beloved is suffering. This is difficult when suffering looks like anger, selfishness, or control. You've got to get good at spotting the pain under the demon. Second, you must be moved by their suffering—you must care. Third, you must be motivated to take action to reduce their suffering. When these three aspects are present, you will find that you are naturally moved to soothe and love your partner, just as you are naturally moved to hug a friend who has just lost their job or to stroke the fur of a frightened kitten. Compassion is the sun under the confusion and control cloud. According to the Buddha, compassion is your natural state. And compassion is an act that fulfills itself—it feels wonderful to act from this state, and when you soothe the pain of the other, you will find you are soothing your own pain, too.

MINDFUL SKILL: Meditation on Kindness and Compassion

This meditation develops feelings of kindness and compassion for yourself and for your partner. You can practice it alone or together.

Seat yourself comfortably and close your eyes. Bring your mind to the experience of being here right now, simply sitting comfortably. Then place your attention at your heart center. Imagine a warm, glowing ball of rose-pink light in your chest. This glowing warmth is soothing, nurturing, and very pleasant. Imagine that it spreads illumination and warmth through your heart. See if you can begin to experience a sense of connection to your heart. You may feel a softening, perhaps a vulnerability, as you invite the heart to glow. Gently, without judgment, imagine you are breathing into the heart center on every inhale and out from the heart center on every exhale. Spend a few moments enjoying breathing into and out from your good, warm heart.

Then, knowing you wish to be happy in life and in love, gently offer the following phrases to your own good heart: "May I be well. My I be happy. May I have a peaceful mind and a happy heart." Repeat these phrases for some time. Next, knowing your partner wishes for the same comfort, bring them to mind. Feel some of your love and care for them, the friendly good feelings. Then repeat: "My sweetheart, may you be well. May you be happy. May you have a peaceful mind and a happy heart."

Next, knowing you wish not to suffer in love, that sometimes you feel angry or selfish or controlling, gently offer to your own good heart: "May I be free from suffering in body and mind. May I be generous, kind, and compassionate." Then for your partner, who doesn't want to suffer in love: "May you be free from suffering in body and mind. May you be generous, kind, and compassionate."

Finally, refresh the warm glow in your heart center and imagine you and your partner together in a state of kind, loving connection. Repeat your heartfelt wish and intention for the two of you to cultivate kindness and compassion. "May we be well. May we be happy. May we have peaceful minds and happy hearts. May we be free from suffering in body and mind and free from suffering in our relationship. May we be generous, kind, and compassionate."

Then allow the phrases to fade away. Feel the warmth and illumination in your heart. Bring a touch of a smile to your lips. Then open your eyes.

Visit http://www.drcherylfraser.com/buddhasbedroom for a guided loving kindness and compassion practice for couples.

Choose Love Now

The Buddha taught that our enemy is our greatest teacher because when we are caught in negative mind states, we get the opportunity to practice wisdom and compassion. So, the love demons are your relationship's greatest teacher, too. When you can spot them, you can change them. If you want to know if the action you are about to take is loving, check the motivation behind it. At its root, is the action motivated by generosity or selfishness, kindness or anger, compassion or control? You know from your own experience that an action feels right when it aligns with your deeper truth, when it is based in open-heartedness, not defensiveness. You can choose love rather than fear and rehearse loving action, deliberately.

So, here is a practical exercise to help you develop the ability to spot the demon and apply the antidote. Because in this very moment, you can focus your mind on the positive, not the negative. You don't need to wait around for your partner to do the right thing in order for you to love them. You can choose to love them right now.

LOVE SKILL: The Dog Biscuit Theory

Have you noticed that your mind often scans for what your mate does wrong instead of what they do right? Let's say you go into the pantry and see they have left the light on … again! What happens next? Do you let the angry demon snap at them, "Hey, remember to turn the light off!" Or do you choose to cultivate kindness and look for something positive rather than focusing on the negative? Next time you notice the offending light, pause for a second or two. Look for something positive to antidote the negative. Perhaps, *My sweetie must have left the light on when they were making the lentil soup.* Now you have a choice. Do you want to focus on the fact that your mate is forgetful about light switches or the fact that they are making your favorite soup for dinner? The choice is yours.

Unfortunately, many of us point out what is wrong and forget to acknowledge what is right. If you want to train your mind, remember how to train a dog. When Fido does something you like, give him a dog biscuit. Reward what you want and ignore what you don't. Use positive reinforcement. The same can apply to love and to your mind. Practice, over and over again, ignoring the demon's voice and searching for the positive. And make it a game: every time you go into the pantry and notice your beloved left the light on, take a few seconds to send some love and sweetness toward them. Form a habit of looking for what your sweetheart does right and commenting on it. Cultivate a mind that is generous, kind, and compassionate. Then act from that loving mind: go give them a hug, tell them they are fabulous, or give them a biscuit.

Love Bytes

♥ Deepen intimacy by changing how you act, speak, and relate with your beloved.

♥ Our defenses don't mean to hurt us. They are trying to keep us safe. Intimacy is not for wimps.

♥ Before you act, check your motivation. Is wisdom-mind or demon-mind urging this action?

♥ Kindness is a choice. You can act nice even when you feel mean. Try it.

Buddha Bytes

🪷 The three roots of suffering are greed, aversion, and confusion. These roots can grow into selfish demon, angry demon, and controlling demon.

🪷 Generosity asks, "What can I do to make you happy?" Generosity gives and receives and fills you both.

🪷 Calm your flooded body so you can calm your angry mind and uncover your kind heart.

🪷 Control freaks always lose. So, let go of the hot coal and allow compassion to flow.

CHAPTER 7

Loving Speech
What Would Buddha Say?

One of the keys to protecting and growing your intimate connection over time is being careful with your speech. Early in your relationship, chances are you spoke kindly and listened attentively. Words were your friends. And your friendly words formed the template for intimacy. Do you remember snuggling under the covers with your new lover, sharing your life stories, revealing secrets, whispering your sexy desires? Yet the very words that in the beginning were tools of love can become weapons over time—it simply depends on how you wield them. Do you still speak as skillfully to your lover as you used to? Sadly, nasty speech, sarcasm, and basic rudeness are prevalent in our culture and, if we are not careful, in our relationship. The last time you went to the grocery store, it's highly probable you heard someone snap at their spouse, "Oh for goodness sake, hurry up! No, we don't *need* any milk. Did you even look in the fridge?" We cringe when we witness couples glare and snipe, but we may speak to our own sweetheart the same way when no one is watching.

"I wish I could take it back," Steven says. The night before, after sharing a long, relaxing stream shower, he rubbed Joleen's feet while they watched a movie. When he slid his hand up her leg to her thigh, she said, "I'm not into sex tonight. I'm really tired." As Steven tells it, he became instantly hurt and angry. He then made the huge mistake of opening his mouth. "I called her an ice queen and said I was sick of being taken for granted. And then I kept going. It's like I'd lost my mind and all I could do was spew these horrible words at her." Joleen was stunned by what he said. She withdrew to the spare room, slept alone, and hadn't spoken to him until just now, sitting on the safe space of my office couch.

No matter how much trust and vulnerability you and your partner cultivate, a few critical, assaultive words can dismantle the intimacy side of your passion triangle. Remember, the source of relationship happiness is acting with open-hearted generosity, kindness, and compassion. We need to speak that way, too. From a mindful loving perspective, the purpose of speech is to bring us closer and increase understanding. In this chapter, you will learn to ask yourself over and over, "How am I speaking to the one I love?" Take it as a heartfelt responsibility to use words to connect you, not drive you apart. Words, and how you share them, are very powerful—so powerful that the Buddha devoted an entire step of the mindful loving path to loving speech.

The Buddha was very precise about how and when to speak. And he set the bar very, very high. He taught that loving speech has five qualities: to be truthful, affectionately spoken, beneficial, spoken at the right time, and motivated by a mind of goodwill. What would it be like if you could apply these five qualities to everything you say? It would mean you only speak the truth—no lies, exaggeration, or verbal trickery. You'd never fib to your spouse or try to manipulate them into going to the opera when you know they don't want to. You would speak in a pleasing, kind, gentle tone of voice. There would be no abusive speech, sharp tone, or mocking inflection. You would evaluate whether or not what you want to say is beneficial in some way. For example, you would ask yourself, Is it useful to point out that they did not put their spoon in the dishwasher? A lot of what we say is better left unsaid. And sometimes, timing is everything. Even the right thing, if said at the wrong time, can create harm. For couples, this means choosing when you will bring up the topic of the overdrawn checking account. Don't mention it three minutes before your spouse has to write their paramedic exam. And don't mention it in the middle of sex, either. Finally, speak only with goodwill—in a manner that promotes harmony in your relationship.

In order to consistently speak like a Buddha, I'd have to tape my mouth shut. I suspect that might be true for you, too. We fail far too often to speak in a loving, helpful, intimate way. But we can practice. Take loving speech as a lifelong training. This may sound like a daunting, if not impossible, task. But mindfulness can help—a lot. By pausing and paying attention to what you are about to say, you can begin to promote more kindness with your choice of words and more compassion in how you speak them.

LOVE SKILL: Touch Before You Talk

When it's time to talk, don't. At least not right away. Just as a picture can be worth a thousand words, sometimes touch speaks volumes. Here is a simple exercise in the loving speech of body language—because sometimes the best conversations are nonverbal.

First, sit facing each other. Then reach out and touch—perhaps put your hand on your partner's leg, intertwine fingers, or gently press your knee against their thigh. Being in touch contact increases intimacy and decreases defensiveness. Simply touching your mate can calm your agitated nervous system and reduce the sense of separation. This can influence you psychologically to feel like a "we" instead of a "you versus me." You may notice that when the conversation gets challenging or difficult, you will want to pull away. But stay in contact. Take the emotional risk of touch.

Then make eye contact. You don't need to stare fixedly at each other by any means, but do make frequent eye contact to show your sweetie that you are here with them, not checking out. And soften your eyes. You can do this volitionally. Try it right now—imagine angry eyes, then imagine kind eyes, and feel the muscles relax. Be aware of your facial expression, too—don't roll your eyes or show signs of dismissiveness. These nonverbal contempt messages create severe turbulence. And don't forget to smile now and then.

Now you are ready for your conversation. Actually, your conversation has already begun, well before any words are spoken. These simple steps of physical connection set you up for success.

Generous Speech and Loving Listening

To be a brilliant communicator, you must be skilled in both verbal and nonverbal speaking—words, tone, and body language. But that is only one lane of the two-lane communication highway—the path from your mind and heart to your partner's mind and heart. You also need to be skilled at receiving their communications to you. Loving speech has to include loving listening. Awakened lovers communicate *with* their beloved, rather than talk *to* them.

Steven prides himself on being a great communicator. "Maybe at work," Joleen says. "His staff say he is a patient and understanding boss. But I don't get that guy at home. He talks and talks, but he doesn't listen to me." The three of us are working to dismantle the hurtful argument of the night before. I want to help this couple discover their triggers so they can watch out for danger zones and prevent future fights. I want them to understand each other's point of view, and I want them to begin to repair the damage that was done. I am teaching them how to communicate with generosity. "Come on, I always communicate with you—I tell you about my day, how I'm feeling, that I missed you. It's you who never asks how I am and gives me the silent treatment as soon as we disagree," Steven gripes.

Steven is making a common—and costly—mistake. He's forgetting that communication is a two-way street. Generous communication is about giving and receiving in equal measure. It's about giving thoughtful, useful words and receiving your partner's words with attentiveness and curiosity. Yes, Steven talks much more than his wife. But he needs to work harder to hear her messages—particularly when he is upset. Last night, when Joleen declined Steven's bid for sex, the selfish demon grabbed his mind and plugged his ears. He lost the ability to listen. Then anger grabbed his tongue, and he used words to attack, to build a wall around his hurting heart so he could feel safe inside it. We all do this—when our body is flooded, we become like a spoiled child covering her ears and saying, "Lalala, I'm not listening." We hurl our words and our needs at our partner. There is only one-way traffic.

Heart-based communicators use words, tone, and body language to bridge the space between and listen with fascination and love. Their motivation isn't to get their point across or win a debate. They want to learn about their partner—this mysterious and fascinating being about whom, ultimately, they know so little. They strive to use speech to understand, to get closer, to build intimacy. Essentially, they have a loving view about the purpose of opening their mouth, and they cherish and protect two-way communication.

Steven would have benefitted from loving listening the other night when his sleepy wife said she was too tired for sex. He could have offered generous words, "I'm disappointed you are too tired for sex, babe, because I've been looking forward to making love with you. For tonight, how about you snuggle into my chest while we fall asleep?" For her part, after his unkind word explosion, Joleen needed to try to understand the hurt under his hostile words by listening with her wisdom, not her ears. There is always a deeper communication within an attack, even though it is delivered in a mean and unfair way. If Joleen heard his loneliness and pain, she may have been able to make a generous offer to reconnect, rather than retreating into silence. "I know you are hurt and angry, but you need to stop saying cruel things. Let's be quiet together. I do love having sex with you. I'm just really worn out from my hospital shift. Let's make a date for sex on Saturday."

Listen with love. Speak with generosity. Generous communicators give more than they get and listen more than they speak. Selfish speech builds walls. Generous speech and loving listening tears them down.

MINDFUL SKILL: How to Be a Great Listener

Loving listening involves giving your attention and open-heartedness and receiving your partner's communication with as much grace and nondefensiveness as you are able. And it takes practice. But it is worth it. For without the capacity to listen with love, all the loving speech in the world falls on closed ears and a walled-off heart.

I invite you to listen to your mate as though honey is coming out of their mouth. Pretend their words are beautiful, meaningful, and very important. Listen with a true heart of curiosity—as though understanding your sweetheart's meaning is of vital importance to you (which, indeed, it should be). Don't just listen with your ears. Listen with your mind, your body, and your heart—with your whole being.

On a practical level, do not interrupt. Don't speak or use facial expressions to derail your beloved from their communication. When your partner pauses, don't rush to fill the space with words. Instead, fill the silence with love and appreciation. Receive their words like an open-hearted, vast pool of curious loving water. And listen, really listen, with mindfulness. Consciously feel your breathing and gently notice if your body or mind are resisting what you are hearing. When you hear something that you disagree with or that creates unpleasant emotion within you, try to soothe yourself and refocus on your partner. Don't mentally rehearse your reply. You are trying to understand your beloved, to experience their side of the clock. Yes, sometimes what they say will be very difficult to hear, but a generous listener truly wants to understand, whether they like the information or not. Practice listening like a friend, not an enemy. And when your sweetheart lets you know that they are finished speaking, thank them for trusting you and for sharing. Then pause and remember love.

If You Can't Say Something Kind, Shut Up

When it comes to speech and intimacy, kindness is key. Loving speech is speech that heals, that brings you closer, that allows you to learn about your partner. Is your speech kind all the time? Probably not. When you are impatient, do you snap with irritation? Do you name-call? Threaten to leave? Are you guilty of speaking with contempt—a major predictor of divorce—toward the one you love? If so, let me reassure you that with effort, you can change your pattern of verbal abuse. But first, you need to own it. "But I was angry! And I said I was sorry later," you wail. But being angry, hurt, or anxious is never an excuse for nasty speech. It's fine to be angry. Emotions happen. They cause a physiological cascade in the body. When you are upset, you can wish you were calm, but you can't change your physiology instantly. However, you can change your speech. And if you are too far gone to change your speech, you need to shut up.

Have you ever had the following experience? You are in the middle of an argument with your partner. Your voice is harsh and loud, and you are saying mean things. Then the phone rings, and you answer in a warm, loving tone, "Hello? Oh, hi! Ben! Lovely to hear from you. What's up?" Because you'd never speak to your friend the way you do to your spouse. Let's face it, if you did, they'd stop being your friend. So, we are entirely capable of sounding nice a split second after we were sounding cruel. Next time you are in the grips of the angry demon, first try the telephone call technique—pretend you are speaking to a friend. Take a moment, make a deliberate choice, and then change your tone and edit your words. This is *applied mindfulness*: bringing conscious awareness to how you sound and what you are saying, then making it kinder. This technique works really well when you hear yourself speaking harshly, provided you are not yet fully flooded. When I explain this to Joleen and Steven, he nods. He says, "I think I'm pretty good at hearing my whiny tone, taking a breath, and speaking more softly a lot of the time. But last night it's like I lost my mind—I kept going and going." Steven is right. Once a flooded person starts talking, it is almost impossible for them to stop. No doubt you have shouted things when you were flooded that you wish you could take back. You rage at your spouse while a small rational part of you observes and thinks, *What the heck am I saying? I must stop! But how?*

In order to speak from kindness, you need to be calm in your body and aware in your mind. If you are too far gone to change your tone and words from ranting to reasonable, you must shut up. Give yourself, and your beloved, the gift of a time-out. You must take a break before you break their heart.

LOVE SKILL: Time-Out Technique for Grown-Ups

Let's say you are arguing, and it starts to escalate. You get edgy, angry, and anxious, and decide you need a time-out because you feel yourself flooding. You believe either you or your partner is at risk of losing control. You or your mate is about to spout something damaging, mean, or contemptuous—or you already have. Follow these steps.

1. Say, "I need a time-out."

2. Both of you must stop talking at that moment. This means no more words. Silence. Complete cessation. In other words, shut up for love. And that includes body language—no sneers, no tossing your hands up in disgust. Remember, this is not an abandonment or a power play to make your partner stop talking. This is a statement of mindful loving. It says, "I know we have to stop or else we are going to hurt our intimacy. We've lost touch with generosity, kindness, and compassion."

3. Look at a timepiece. A time-out lasts precisely thirty minutes. It takes at least twenty minutes for a flooded, agitated physiology to calm down and for the mind to

become reasonable again—so give yourself thirty before you try to speak.

4. During the thirty-minute, silent time-out, calm yourself as best you can. This is where you self-soothe, as you learned in the previous chapter. Create space for your system to settle. Do not use this break to tell yourself negative, self-righteous stories: *This is all their fault; they are so selfish; they never care about my needs.* Those types of thoughts feed the demons and will re-flood your system. The purpose of the time-out is to calm the body and mind, not rev it up all over again.

5. In exactly thirty minutes, come back together. If you have followed the instructions, you should be relatively calm and somewhat rational now. You can decide together how you want to reunite after a time-out— discuss this once you have reviewed these instructions. Some couples like to hug. Others just say, "Hi." Some say, "I'm sorry things got heated." One husband I know grins a goofy grin to break the ice and reconnect with his wife. This coming together is meant to say, "I still love you, and we are not our stories." Even if you are still angry, hurt, or frightened, you acknowledge with your presence that you've honored the time-out. You may or may not be ready to talk about the hot button issue. But you've prevented a nasty, destructive argument.

The time-out stops the carnage. If you practice this technique and it becomes a reliable tool, you never have to have a damaging, pointless argument ever again. Really. Now a reality check: the time-out is very difficult to master. But commit to practicing this technique, and gradually you will get better at it. Together, you can get to the point where the time-out technique is your relationship's best friend.

Compassionate Communication

What's the dumbest argument you've ever had with a partner? Mine happened in a little blue convertible, driving to my former boy-friend's cabin. We were in love, but we clashed often. We stopped for ice cream, and he brought me the wrong flavor. I complained loudly; he fired back. Then he reached over, took the sundae, and threw it out of the moving car. I stared at him in open-mouthed shock. A cascade of nasty words rushed toward my mouth. Then I had a flash of insight into his experience—he'd tried to please me, I'd criticized, he felt rejected. My heart opened a little. In that moment I had a choice. I could keep criticizing, or I could contact my heart and speak with compassion toward the man I loved. So, I chose to let go of control, of wanting what I wanted, and accept reality. Right flavor or wrong flavor, the ice cream was gone. So, I laughed, he relaxed, and I pledged to learn to fight fair.

In order to fight fair, you need to have loving view and let go of trying to control your mate. Remember, there is another point of view. For harmony and deep intimacy, you must truly want to under-stand your partner—how they feel and think, not bully them into seeing things as you do and doing things the way you want. When you are feeling anxious or hurt during an argument, you're having a physiological reaction coupled with a mental story: *He never listens to me. What kind of moron mistakes chocolate for hot fudge?* But these temporary thoughts are not real. You are defending your point of view against your perceived enemy—you know, the person you love when you are not triggered. You've lost compassion and are trying to control reality, all the while forgetting there is another reality right now—that of your partner. What would happen if you got curious? If you made space to deeply listen to your beloved and to ask them to deeply listen to you? So, the next time you are arguing, ask your-self: Is there really something to fight about? Or are your arguments all in your head? Sadly, many things we argue about are no more substantial than the imagined monster under your childhood bed. If you listen to your mate and attempt to understand instead of lashing out, the issue that seemed so vital can be seen for the illusion it is. Love demons dissolve in the flashlight of understanding and compassion. Compassionate communication replaces confusion with clarity, and distance with connection.

When Steven rubbed Joleen's thigh, she said she didn't want sex, and they argued, there were two different realities present, two sides of the clock, and then nasty words and damaged intimacy. In mere seconds, they were in separate rooms nursing their wounds, their stories, and their distance. But Joleen and Steven are determined to become better communicators, and so far, they have improved in several areas. They are both working hard to soothe themselves when their demons grab hold and to take a time-out when needed. They are trying to listen skillfully. Now they are ready to apply these skills in my favorite communication exercise.

MINDFUL SKILL: I Truly Care about Your Side of the Clock"

This powerful technique is actually quite simple. I suggest you use it after an argument to deepen your understanding of what went wrong. It is also terrific for discussing topics you disagree about or tend to avoid. This compassionate communication exercise trains you to be a better speaker and listener. But note that this is not about reaching a conclusion or solving a problem—not yet. This is about making sure both you and your beloved feel respected and understood. (You may wish to review The Other Side of the Clock love skill in chapter 4 before you begin.)

1. Choose your topic. Then block off thirty minutes. Sit down, ready to communicate, to get closer, and to learn. Take three mindful breaths. Touch. Flip a coin to decide who begins.

2. Joleen and Steven debrief their recent argument. Steven speaks first. He gets exactly ten minutes. He uses his time to explain as thoroughly as he can what his experience was: How he felt close to Joleen after their shower, he loved rubbing her feet, he got turned on and thought it would be beautiful to make love. How rejected and hurt he felt when she said no. What his thoughts and emotions were. How ashamed he feels for the cruel things he said. All of it. For ten uninterrupted minutes, his job is to thoroughly explain his perspective. Joleen's task is to listen with love, to be attentive, and to receive his meaning as best she can.

   Here are a few rules: The speaker can say anything they want to help the listener understand their experience, but they cannot speak in a cruel manner. The listener must not interrupt—use all the loving listening skills you learned earlier. The listener can use a notepad if they wish, if it helps them to jot down the main points the speaker is sharing (this becomes useful in the second step, where the listener will sum up what the speaker said).

3. The listener, Joleen, is now asked to sum up what she heard her partner say. Now, for this summary, it is important to only summarize what you heard. No interpretations, no opinions, no embellishment. Be a loving reporter, dealing in facts. Joleen says, "So, what I got from your perspective is that you were relaxed and feeling loving and horny on the couch. You really miss me, and you miss making love, so when you touched my thigh and I pulled away, you felt super hurt and disappointed. Then you got really angry and said those mean things." Summing up what your partner said is a critical step in compassionate communication. It lets your

partner know that *you hear them*. That you really are paying attention, that you cherish their experience, that you want to understand them deeply. This step validates your partner's reality—letting them know you accept it even if you don't agree.

4. The speaker lets the listener know if they feel understood. Steven says, "Yes, I feel like you got the main points I said; thank you." If he feels Joleen's summary missed a major chunk of what he shared, he can say, "You got some of it, but I don't feel that you are clear on how hurt I was."

That's it. I share; you summarize; I let you know if I feel understood. Then we switch, and you speak for ten minutes—in this case, Joleen would explain her experience of the argument, what her thoughts and feelings were. Steven listens and takes notes if it helps him pay attention. Steven summarizes her perspective, and she lets him know if he got it. Then they say thank you and, if it feels right, share a hug.

You Break It, You Fix It—Together

So, you are committed to being a compassionate communicator. But you are not perfect. Let's face it. Even healthy, happy couples argue—and sometimes they fight dirty. Despite the hard work you put into your relationship, despite the hours logged on the meditation cushion, and certainly despite your best and most loving intentions, you won't always handle relationship conflict well. Even as fledgling awakened lovers, we all mess up sometimes. Some of these mistakes are foolish and unintentional. But sometimes we launch targeted attacks on our mate's vulnerability. We cause harm to our partner and to the intimacy between us. So, what do you do when your demons win and you wound with words?

Apologize. Don't ignore the mistakes—if you don't tend to hurts, they can accumulate. Unacknowledged wounds can feed mind demons and build walls between you. In terms of mindful loving, our mistakes are our greatest teachers. Every unskillful act or word gives us the opportunity to begin again. When you fail at loving speech, I recommend you take a love mulligan. In golf, some players allow themselves a do-over after a lousy shot, a second chance to make it right. This works great in love, too. When the damage has been done, skillful couples make a repair and start over. Awakened lovers are not perfect, but they are committed to generosity, kindness, and compassion. When they get stuck in a sand trap, they are determined to dig themselves out, learn something, and do better the next time around.

To give or receive a good apology is an art—and a good apology takes two people. There is the giver and the receiver. The apology must be offered, and it must be accepted. An apology that heals is based in kindness, generosity, and compassion. I've hurt you. I realize it. I feel moved by your suffering, and out of compassion, I want to remove your suffering. As the offender, *I offer you my repair.* I apologize with a kind heart, voice, and words. I attempt to renew our intimacy. But I cannot repair alone. Even an apology crafted by the Buddha himself is not complete unless the recipient accepts it with grace and offers something in return: forgiveness. When you have hurt me, I see you struggle. I know your demons won that round, that you feel badly about what you said, and I feel compassion for your suffering. I hear your apology with a kind heart, ears, and mind. *And then I forgive you.* Without my forgiveness, our rift cannot heal.

So, we, offender and offended, bear equal responsibility for bringing together that which was torn asunder. We are lovers, together. In fact, from a mindful loving perspective, our relationship is something we each bear, not partial, but full responsibility for. My mind causes my unhappiness, not you. So even when you've said something cruel, I can choose, with my mind, to let it go—to see beyond the temporary clouds to the shining sun of love and awakening underneath. So yes, my love, I forgive you. I forgive you for your humanity, your flaws, your missteps. I see the beautiful being you are, and I am here to offer you my hand and help you step out of the confusion and into the clarity. And I ask you to do the same for me when I fail.

LOVE SKILL: Mindful Apology—Repair, Forgive, Begin Again

Repair: Here is a repair manual for when your mouth has betrayed your deeper heart and the demon got your tongue. "I'm sorry" is a good start, but for an apology to rebuild intimacy, it should have three qualities. If you have said something unfair, first you need to own the mistake. Second, you need to repair the damage. Third, you need to vow to improve.

So, practice saying, "I'm sorry" in the form own, repair, improve. I did X (own), I'm sorry (repair), and I'm going to do Y (improve). It might sound something like this: "Sweetheart, I want to acknowledge that I said I hate going to see you play ball and that sports are a waste of time. That was a mean thing to say [own]. Sometimes I'm selfish about my time, and that's not fair to you. I'm sorry I said that [repair]. Next time you ask me come to a game, I'm going to say yes [improve]." You can include some humor for bonus points: "But hey, let's be real, you married an artist who can't throw a ball, what do you expect? I love you, babe."

The template is simple, but you will likely need to practice. If you are like me, you will get a lot of opportunity to practice—even experts mess up.

Forgive: Can you "forgive and forget"? If you have been hurt, you may never completely forget. But you can always forgive because forgiveness is a choice—a choice you may need to make over and over again. When your troublesome mind seizes on something your partner said or did that hurt you, you've forgotten the present moment. You are reliving something that no longer exists—that moment this morning when they said that mean thing. You are creating your own suffering here and now. Unless you can choose to forgive your beloved, you cannot dance in the present moment with them. You are tainted by the past. By choosing to forgive them, you are also choosing to forgive yourself, for you make mistakes too. Choose to stop creating pain in this perfect moment.

"I forgive you" is a good start to accepting an apology. But for loving speech, I recommend three steps for the receiver, as well. First, thank your partner for caring so much about you and your relationship. Second, acknowledge that your partner has owned their mistake and is attempting to repair it. Then third, accept the apology.

So practice saying, "I forgive you," in the form thank, acknowledge, accept. Thank you for saying X (thank), I appreciate you owning what you said (acknowledge), and I forgive you for Y (accept). It might sound something like this: "Thanks for saying that [thank]. It did piss me off when you were rude about my baseball game. I felt like you aren't interested in the sport I love. It takes guts to admit you were mean [acknowledge]. It's okay. I accept your apology. I'd love you to come to the game Wednesday [accept]." You can include humor here too for bonus points for a counter offer that acknowledges the partner's side of the clock: "And hey, maybe we can go for drinks after at the weird art café you like!"

Begin Again: Unfinished business accumulates. Let go of the small slights and the large wounds so they don't pile up and obscure the sun. Practice dual apologies often. I'm sorry. I forgive you. And now we begin again, as friends, as lovers, in this moment. Step by step, together, as we become passion.

Love Bytes

♥ Loving speech brings you closer. Words can be tools of love or weapons of hurt. Wield them wisely.

♥ Generous communicators give more than they get and listen more than they speak. They strive to understand, not just be understood.

♥ If you can't say something kind, shut up. Practice time-outs. Take a break before you break your beloved's heart.

♥ Apology is an art, and it takes two. Together, you can repair, forgive, and begin again.

Buddha Bytes

☸ Every time you open your mouth, you have an opportunity to engage in a mindfulness practice.

☸ What would Buddha say? Whatever he said, it would be truthful, affectionately spoken, beneficial, timely, and motivated by goodwill.

☸ Learn to speak with your beloved, rather than talk to them. Communication is a two-way street.

☸ Compassionate communication replaces confusion with clarity and distance with connection.

CHAPTER 8

Loving Livelihood
Make Your Love Life a Hobby

When you committed to your partner, you signed a lifelong contract for the job. How seriously are you taking this commitment? Do you put in the minimum work so you don't get fired, then escape to do the things you love to do the minute the whistle blows? The fifth step on the eightfold path of mindful loving is based on what the Buddha called *right livelihood*. He gave teachings on how to engage fully and compassionately with your work life—be that a job, career, parenting, or volunteering. In *Buddha's Bedroom*, your livelihood is your relationship.

In essence, "I do" means "You're hired." Sadly, too many people do end up treating their relationship like an obligation—putting in time just to get a small emotional or sexual paycheck—instead of investing in the wondrous journey and reaping the rewards. For relationship can be the path to awakening—a tough but profoundly rewarding path—if you walk it with mindfulness. Nothing else will challenge your equilibrium as much as love and passion do. As you well know, your love relationship brings you face-to-face with your demons, your clinging, your suffering, and your own mind in a dramatic manner. And by doing so, it provides ample opportunities to practice generosity, kindness, and compassion—toward your beloved and toward yourself. So, if you want to develop your patience and clarity "love muscles" and practice the skills needed for true, lifelong intimacy, take relationship as your loving livelihood.

I bet you try hard to be good at your job. And by reading this book and doing the exercises, you are trying hard to be good at your relationship. Ironically, however, treating your love life like a job is bound to backfire. Let's face it. No one wants to have to "work on" their relationship. So, get that idea out of your head. Change your view. Mindful loving is driven by the inner desire to cultivate passion, not an obligation imposed by the external boss. Don't make your relationship a grind. Approach passion with a more playful and lighthearted attitude. Make it a priority to cultivate romance, fun, and novelty in your relationship. Commit to becoming a great lover. Meet your beloved with curiosity. Bring interest and excitement back into the humdrum you have allowed to leach into the places where passion used to play. If you want loving livelihood, don't "work on" your relationship. Instead, treat your love life like a hobby.

Love Like It's Your Hobby

Can your love life be a hobby? You bet it can. In fact, I teach couples that the best way to strengthen their emotional and sexual connection is to treat their love life like they do their golf game or pottery skills. Think about it. What makes something a hobby? A hobby is an activity or interest undertaken for pleasure or relaxation. You pursue your hobby by choice, not out of obligation. You don't get paid for it. You make it a priority and carve out time to pursue it. You plan for it, and you look forward to it. What's more, you practice your hobby and strive to improve, hoping to master your chosen pursuit. What a beautiful teaching of how to approach your long-term relationship. So, how can you make your love life your hobby?

First, remember that love is fun. You enjoy your hobby. Dates with your mate should also be pleasurable. Instead of feeling resentful when your sweetie pesters you into taking them bowling, cultivate a new attitude and find pleasure in spending time with them. Loosen up. Find the humor in your mate's annoying habits. Laugh more often. And make sex a hobby, too. After all, the word "foreplay" includes the word "play." Recreate some of the joy, delight, and lust you and your beloved enjoyed when you were dating. The more you practice your love hobby, the richer your relationship will be.

Second, make your love life a priority. You say you really want a profound love affair, but are you walking that talk? You go to hockey practice or scrapbooking class because it matters to you, but you may let romance and sex fall way down your priority list. Think about the last week. What did you spend most of your time and energy on? Sadly, many couples invest very few hours in their relationship— unless they make passion a priority. I fell into the trap of forgetting to prioritize passion myself last year. I used to give my man foot rubs while we watched a movie, but I hadn't oiled his toes in months. We used to set the alarm twenty minutes early so we could have a sweet and hot morning quickie, but we'd substituted snooze for shag. But once we noticed our love life needed some help, my sweetie and I rebooted things and made romance, love, and sex a priority again. The slippery massage oil now lives on the coffee table, a small reminder to slow down and pay attention to touch. And yes, the morning quickie has returned. Not all by itself—we cannot count on that raging arousal of our early months together—but because we decide to make love happen and set an early alarm. And boy, is it worth it. Things feel fun again. Our relationship feels more like a hobby than an obligation. Just like you plan your annual vacation, poring over beach photos and salivating over scuba diving packages, plan a hot romantic weekend for next month and savor the anticipation. This can increase thrill and make your love life more interesting and electric.

Third, decide to improve at your hobby and vow to become a better lover. Improving at anything takes intention, planning, and action. So, make a commitment to developing your mindful loving skills. But don't fall into the trap of striving for a specific end result. The mindful loving path is not linear, nor is it meant to be a grim slog. Rather, there are eight qualities to develop, to explore, and to experience. Enjoy the path itself, not just the so-called destination. Cultivate love for the process of relating. Explore passion for exploration's sake. Of course, you want to improve and to be more playful, sexy, kind, and generous together, but can you also enjoy whatever is happening right now? Treat your connection as what it is—a living, breathing, changing dynamic that thrives on attention and effort but deteriorates when ignored or taken for granted. Like great gardens, great relationships need tending. Treating you love life like a hobby helps you bring curiosity, presence, and passion to your lover and to the intimate connection between you. Start right now. Prioritize your love affair and take action. Plan for passion. Carve out time to go for a hike and talk about life, study tantric sex, and bring a spirit of fun and exploration to your relationship. And remember how to play.

LOVE SKILL: Your Passion Plan

Each of you is going to create a passion plan. Come up with some daily, weekly, and monthly relationship commitments for the year ahead. You can draw from the exercises and tools we've gone through so far. For example, you might commit to a kiss every morning, a sexy shower every night, or to practicing mindfulness for thirty minutes. Weekly commitments may include daily things like practicing The Other Side of the Clock communication exercise, scheduling time to give your sweetie a massage, or making love every Wednesday and Sunday. Monthly commitments might include setting aside a whole day for connection, fun, and romance. Plan to explore something you haven't done before. You might go to a salsa dancing club, take a free class, and then stay for the evening shimmy. Or perhaps you will go zip lining, and then try the new Irish pub for dinner. Make it a technology-free day—no cell phones, no Internet, no distractions. Pay full attention to each other. And though we haven't gotten there yet in this book, don't forget the sensuality part of your relationship. You will get plenty of ideas in the following chapters for sexy daily, weekly, and monthly activities. Begin your passion plan today, with the skills you've learned so far, and then add to it as you progress through the book and for the rest of your life. Keep it fresh and fun.

Don't just think about this exercise casually. Take action. Your passion plan needs to be written down. Once you have created it, take time to share your ideas with your partner. Then you can come up with your shared passion plan. Incorporate at least one daily, weekly, and monthly suggestion from each of your individual plans. Then print a copy of your passion plan and post it in your bedroom. It's time to take action and make your love life a hobby.

Pay Attention, for Passion's Sake

I watch the couple on my couch and smile. Joleen tilts her head and nods thoughtfully as Steven speaks. She reaches out with a finger and touches his inner wrist, cuing him that she'd like to reply. I am watching a different version of the pair who first came to me in such distress, on the verge of divorce. Their relationship has evolved from a miserable job to an enjoyable hobby. They are better able to spot the mind demons and to apply the antidotes. They practice compassionate communication—calling a time-out when they are flooded, listening deeply, and validating each other. And this week they've started working with their passion plan. All this effort put in to the hobby of loving mindfully is paying off. They are pleased to see each other at the end of the day; some thrill energy has returned. They are connecting in an intimate way again; they are curious and kind, like the friends they used to be. The couples therapy has clearly been helpful. But there is one other key thing that has helped improve how they act and speak with each other. They meditate. Sometimes they meditate together; sometimes separately. But they have each committed to what I call a "daily-ish" mindfulness practice—they hit the cushion a minimum of four or five times a week for thirty minutes. As I watch them on my couch, the main thing that has changed is that they are paying attention.

To be a great lover, you must pay attention and notice your partner trying to connect with you. It takes presence to notice your partner glancing your way during a dinner party. According to John Gottman, master of marriage research, successful couples are mindful of bids for connection and pay attention to them. These bids might be a look, a question, or an affectionate stroke on the cheek, anything that says, "Hey, I want to be connected with you." Most bids happen in simple, mundane ways, and if you are mindless, you miss the overture. Gottman's studies indicate that couples on the road to divorce ignore their spouse's bids for connection 50 to 80 percent of the time, while those in happy marriages catch most of these emotional cues and respond kindly. So, paying attention predicts relationship success. Couples who notice more moments of connection report more feelings of love and contentment. What's more, connection and intimacy buffer against emotional burnout. If you are not paying attention, you won't notice your distressed partner reaching out with a sigh or a question, and you sure can't respond to the bids you miss. And it turns out these failed intimacies are as harmful as active rejection—simply not acknowledging your mate hurts as much as a harsh word. One of my clients calls being unnoticed by his wife "death by a thousand cuts." A bid for attention is a request, and paying attention so you can catch and respond to the bid is a gift given with an open heart.

This is one way meditation makes you a better partner. If you practice mindfulness, you become more aware. You learn to really notice what each breath feels like and to discern subtle changes in your mind and body. You experience what is actually happening, rather than escaping into distraction. When your mind does lose attention, you practice refocusing on the present. And off the meditation cushion, in your life and particularly in your relationship, meditation strengthens your ability to slow down so you can show up—to look with fresh eyes, to listen with fresh ears, to develop your partner radar so you regularly notice your partner reaching out, and to respond with kindness and interest. With practice, you can move from mindless and preoccupied to actively seeing your mate and their needs, just like Steven and Joleen did. And this matters. Mindful couples are happy couples. The simple, mundane moments of connection build intimacy and happiness. Without mindful awareness, the intimacy side of your triangle will grow weak, and passion will languish. Whether in thought, word, or deed, mindfulness is the key to intimacy, thrill, and sensuality. So, pay attention, for passion's sake.

MINDFUL SKILL: Daily Mindful Loving Meditation

For twenty minutes each morning (or at any time), practice the following meditation on mindful loving.

1. State an aspiration. For example, "Today, may I think, speak, and act toward my beloved with as much generosity, kindness, and compassion as I am able."

2. Bring your attention to your feet. Ground yourself in the body. Slowly scan your body from feet to head, connecting with it and gently observing it.

3. Bring your attention to your breath. Invite the mind to settle. Using the breath as the meditation object, practice mindfulness for approximately five minutes. If the mind wanders, gently refocus on the breath.

4. Slowly bring your attention to the day ahead. Scan through the day to come: your plans, obligations, intentions. Where does your love relationship fit into your day today? Select one or two positive, wholesome love priorities. Perhaps decide to skip your favorite TV show so you can make your mate a lovely meal. Don't overthink it—trust whatever arises and feels like a loving relationship priority for the day to come.

5. Mentally review your passion plan and recommit to your daily commitments.

6. Place your palm on your heart and take three breaths into and out from your heart center. Bring to mind three things you appreciate about your beloved.

7. Allow all that to fade away and take one more mindful breath.

8. Repeat your aspiration.

9. Create a mindful loving day, regardless of circumstances.

Visit http://www.drcherylfraser.com/buddhasbedroom for a guided version of this practice and further teachings.

LOVE SKILL: The Three-Breath Hug Hello

The key turns in the lock, and I hear, "Hey." My sweetheart is home. Without getting up from my writing chair, I say, "Hey," back. Meanwhile, our dogs tumble over each other in a delighted rush around the corner to the front door, where they leap, lick, and wag their love and appreciation. Mindful loving scorecard: dogs 1, Cheryl 0. So, my guy and I make a pledge to bring some presence into our greetings. You can, too. Make coming together a moment of mindfulness, a chance to truly pay attention to each other. Reunions matter. Each time you see your beloved, whether you've been apart for an hour or a week, you have an opportunity to begin anew. Make each greeting a celebration of the present moment and the connection between you.

So, for the next month, practice this hug hello: When you hear your partner at the door, get up and go to them. Make eye contact. Smile. Then wrap them in a hug, your chest pressing against their chest. Literally create a heartfelt embrace. Then breathe in together, deeply. Imagine breathing in peace and calm. Breathe out together. Imagine letting go of any tension or fatigue. Repeat three times. This simple practice brings intimacy and attention to your greeting. It calms your physiology and moves you out of your head and into your body. Your heart rate will slow. Psychologically, you will begin to transition from "there" to "here," from "that" to "this," from "apart" to "together." If you are feeling frisky, once you have completed your three-breath hug, you can always leap, lick, and wag your tail.

When the Love Song Ends— Quit or Commit?

Why is intimate connection something we crave so much? In a word, impermanence. The Buddha's teaching is here to bite your butt and remind you that everything changes. When we first hear them, the four facts of life are terrifying. They say that our strategies are doomed to fail. That nothing lasts forever. True safety, true refuge, can only come from within. But before we embrace the four facts, we truly believe we can create external security—something permanent and satisfying to stave off the winds of change. We desperately crave something that feels solid. That's why we commit to one person, buy that house to put our relationship inside, and swear to love each other till death do us part. In our confusion, we believe a relationship is the answer to dukkha. Everything will be okay now that we've found each other—just like the love songs say.

But nothing could be further from the truth. In love, we kind of do everything wrong, in terms of Dharma and freedom from suffering. After all, clinging creates suffering, right? And where else do we cling anywhere near as hard, anywhere near as desperately, as to our mate? Don't leave me. Don't look at another woman or man. Don't lock me out of your private thoughts. Don't forget to call me, tell me you love me, smile at me when I feel low, or put a quarter of a teaspoon of brown sugar in my latte. And whatever you do, don't die before I do. Be here for me, keep me happy.

Sorry, love songs, but we commit to each other for the wrong reasons. And that's not romantic at all. At first, we crave commitment to guarantee love and security. The conundrum is that the very thing we grab to make us feel secure—a romantic relationship—is inherently changeable and cannot deliver the never-ending happiness we crave. Then, when we start to wake up to reality, we question our commitment and are adrift in doubt. Our relationship isn't so interesting and fun anymore, and it's not doing its job—protecting us from suffering. Let's face it, when their livelihood stops satisfying them, a lot of people start looking for a better job. Same is true with love. A lifelong commitment is dissolved with a stroke of a judge's pen. Then you are off, looking for love in all the wrong places again. Both of these states are based in confusion—the belief that your spouse can keep you happy and the belief that it is their fault you are miserable. The first confusion goes like this: "I love you! Marry me! Keep me happy!" The second confusion sounds like, "I'm not happy. You are the reason. I'm leaving." And then this happens: "When I find spouse number two, it'll all be okay. Hey, new partner, I love you! Marry me! Keep me happy!" And so it goes.

So, when the going gets tough in your relationship, remember the facts of life and decide to change your mind, not your mate. Instead of letting go of your relationship, explore letting go of your belief that you can find happiness outside of yourself. Yes, commitment is terrifying because we know it cannot last. But if you are willing to face the fear of eventual loss, you can cultivate the deep intimacy that comes from vulnerability. Yes, your relationship hobby will be really, really tough sometimes. But if you quit, you will never master mindful loving.

Loving You No Matter What

A Dharma student asked me recently, "So, do Buddhists believe there is no point to marriage?" Essentially, since everything is impermanent and we cannot find lasting happiness in a relationship, why commit to anyone, ever? I suggested that if we commit to someone with loving view—seeing the truth of reality, knowing our mate is not our soulmate—we can take relationship as a mindful loving path. We can walk side by side and assist each other to live a compassionate, joyful, meaningful life within the truths of old age, sickness, and death. When you see the truth of impermanence and embrace it, as well as embracing your mate, you create the possibility of a deep and profound intimacy. Choosing to commit from wisdom instead of neediness and confusion can give a greater meaning to your love life. Precisely because you know that it cannot last forever, you realize that your time together is short and precious. Therefore, you start to love more mindfully. You choose to face the burden of impermanence with four shoulders, not two. You understand that your sweetheart cannot make you happy all the time, and that helps you honor and appreciate your relationship rather than trying to simply satisfy your own desires. Loving livelihood can give you a sense of purpose, calm, and stability based in something larger than you. You desire to explore the mystery you call your spouse. You catch a glimmer of the limitless opportunities to learn about them, to touch them in a new way, and to share sorrows and delights. And you can fall in love again, over and over, with the one you are already with.

In this moment now, whenever you're reading these words, are you fully "in" with your partner? Sure, you may be married and have no intention of breaking up. But are you really giving everything you have to your beloved and to your relationship? I'm going to challenge you, invite you, and hopefully provoke you to make a choice to commit 100 percent of yourself to your relationship today. Notice how this invitation impacts you. If you're frightened by the idea of committing 100 percent in this moment, find out why. Do you have doubts about your relationship? Do you focus on what is missing and the needs your partner does not fulfill instead of what works? Do you fear your partner cannot commit to you? Or are you one of the many people who have a little bit of yourself reserved for someone else, someone better, maybe even your soulmate, who may come along? Don't beat yourself up if that is true. My pesky mind demons make me doubt my relationship, too. But having 10 percent of my mind open to something other than what is present is not mindful loving—it is mindless loving. Commitment is a head trip. Remember how your curiosity about your partner, your level of intrigue, and your boredom are up to you and your mind? The same is true with commitment. Your level of commitment isn't about a wedding ring or whether you finally bought a house and both of your names are on the mortgage papers. Your level of commitment is completely contained in your own mind. Marriage vows and mortgages fall apart if your mind isn't 100 percent committed.

So here is an idea: Commit to your mate again, but this time, from clarity instead of confusion, and from acceptance instead of clinging. The first time, you probably chose your mate for the wrong reasons. This second time can be for the right reasons. So, when you are mired in doubts and questioning your commitment, instead of contemplating leaving, can you practice simply being with what is? Rather than indulging the hope that someone better is out there, plant your feet and stay. Choose to face reality even when it is painful and let go into this relationship with this person right now. Your mate cannot meet all your needs. Stop trying to get that which is impossible. Loving livelihood requires sticking the course and discovering that it is possible to find passion and grace in the midst of the ups and downs of life by choosing to stay with whatever is happening and practicing generosity, kindness, and compassion. And that deepens intimacy. "I love you, and I am here to grow with you, no matter what."

MINDFUL SKILL: 100 Percent Commitment, One Day at a Time

I invite you to commit completely to your partner right now, in a new way. I'm challenging you to remove the escape clause. To make that easier to do, doubts and all, you are going to make a rock-solid, diamond-plated commitment to your beloved for *today*. To put this into action, decide how you want to word your commitment. Then write it down and sign it. Once you have created your commitment, share it with your partner. Ask them if they are also willing to commit fully to the relationship for today. Then, read your vows out loud to each other every morning.

When I invited Joleen and Steven to recommit and to share daily vows, they came up with the following:

> I, Joleen, on this day, commit 100 percent of my heart, my mind, and myself to you, my partner, Steven, the "imperfect person I love." I commit to being with you through the ups and downs. Frankly, sometimes I have doubts about us, honey. But today I am committing completely to learning to fix our issues and to bringing passion back. Together, we're going to find the way. I commit to being more patient, to speaking more kindly, and to touching you often. I commit to trying to keep my heart open when I feel scared. Today, I will love you no matter what. You can count on me.

> I, Steven, on this day, commit 100 percent of my heart, my mind, and myself to you, my partner, Joleen, the "imperfect person I love." I commit to listening to you deeply, to being strong for you when you need me, and to seeing the beautiful woman you are. I commit to calming my fears when I'm anxious and asking for a hug instead of

acting from neediness and selfishness. I commit to a big kiss and embrace hello when you come home and to making time for romance. Today, I will love you no matter what. You can count on me.

Committing for just for one day will help you defeat your fears and love demons by limiting the commitment to here and now. This is a vow far more important than the marriage vow you may have made in the beginning when your reasons to commit were confused. Renew your commitment daily with this new, thoughtful vow. And don't let it become habitual. Revise it frequently; keep it alive, evolving, and real. Your daily vow is a beautiful, loving livelihood commitment based in wisdom, acceptance, and clarity. One that gently reminds you to stick with your relationship hobby, even when it's really tough. It supports you to love with presence, no matter what, one day, one moment, one breath at a time.

Love Bytes

- 💜 "I do" means "You're hired." Make your loving livelihood a path to awakening.

- 💜 Treating your love life like a job will backfire. Instead of "working on" your relationship, make your love life a hobby.

- 💜 It's never too late to make passion a priority once again. Plan for passion, create romance, and study to become a better lover.

- 💜 Commit to your partner from clarity, not confusion. Vow to love them fully, one day at a time, no matter what.

Buddha Bytes

- 🪷 Your love life should be fun. Approach your relationship, and your partner, with a more playful, curious mind.

- 🪷 Commit to a daily-ish mindful loving meditation: "Today, may I think, speak, and act toward my beloved mate with as much generosity, kindness, and compassion as I am able."

- 🪷 Mindful couples are happy couples who catch bids for connection. So, pay attention, for passion's sake.

- 🪷 Awakened lovers explore multiple ways of relating with their sweetheart—they know loving well is not something you master; it is a dynamic exploration.

PART IV

SENSUALITY

THE MINDFUL
LOVING PATH

CHAPTER 9

Loving Mindfulness
Slowing Your Mind Is
Great Foreplay

People often ask me what sex and meditation have to do with each other. A lot! Fully experiencing the moment applies to both sitting on a cushion in mindfulness meditation and to touching your lover, as well as everything in between. As you've seen so far, the path of mindful loving starts with changing your view and setting intentions to reignite thrill, and then moves to cultivating loving speech and behavior to deepen intimacy. Now it's time to turn to the third side of the passion triangle, sensuality. Sensuality is a powerful, beautiful, and necessary part of being an awakened lover. And you don't notice sensation if you are not paying attention.

Imagine meditating on something as simple as a raisin. Explore it with your senses with focus and curiosity. Truly see its wrinkly beauty, smell vineyards and sunlight, caress it with your tongue, hear a slight sigh as you bite down, and taste the flood of sweet liquid release. Mmm. Well, you just made love with that raisin. When you bring that level of full sensual curiosity to your sweetheart, you are a way better lover. After all, typical long-term-relationship sex is the antithesis of mindful. We shove the present moment aside in a rush to the finale, escape into sexual fantasy, and focus on what we get rather than what we give. With mindful sensuality, the invitation is to slow down, explore the moment as it is, focus intently on what we are directly experiencing, and exchange profound emotional and sensory communion. By paying deep attention to our lover's body and heart as well as our own, we discover that arousal is just the beginning. Sexual meditation can create both transcendent mind states and intense pleasure—including multiple, extended, and full-body orgasms. But to be successful at awakened lovemaking, you need a mind that can slow down and show up and a body that can experience pleasure with presence. Ultimately, as with every other experience you have, great sex is all in your head. And mindfulness helps you minimize distractions by staying focused on what's actually happening (I'm here in bed with you, kissing ... not sending that email that's been on my mind), by paying close attention (I'm experiencing the touch of your fingertips on my thigh ... mmm), and by becoming more self-aware (I'm really enjoying connecting with you sexually and emotionally). So, sex and meditation have a lot to do with each other. If you want to have more, and better, sex, mindful loving is key. Combining sensuality and loving mindfulness is simply sensational.

LOVE SKILL: Touch More, Touch Often

Mindfulness involves observing and experiencing the present moment with all five senses and with the mind itself. Sensuality involves the whole body, not just the sexual erogenous zones. Touching your beloved can get you out of your head and into your body here and now in the present moment. So, touch more, and touch often. Of course, we will be talking a great deal about sexual touch in the chapters in this section, but touch is best practiced all day long. Touching more instead of relying too much on words will help you be a more generous, kind, and compassionate partner. Dacher Keltner of the Greater Good Science Center calls touch "the primary language of compassion." Touch is related to physiological processes that promote relaxation, health, and well-being. Touch calms cardiovascular stress, triggers oxytocin (the "love hormone"), and activates the vagus nerve. As a couple, touching calms us and brings us closer, bridging the gap between us. Two separate bodies and minds, me and you, become an "us" when we embrace.

Take a pledge for intimate touch practice. For the next seven days, explore a variety of ways you can use touch to connect with your lover when you are not making love. In addition to hugging hello, add a passionate kiss good-bye—with tongue. Hold hands at the table; massage feet while you watch a movie; place your hand on the back of their neck as they drive. Shower together as often as possible, and soap each other's bodies with reverence and focus. Sleep naked, and spoon or cuddle with your head on your partner's chest for at least five minutes before you fall asleep. Spend five minutes cuddling in the morning before you leap out of bed. Next, review your passion plan and add more touch practices. Make connecting with your bodies part of your daily life together. Try it. Discover. Explore. Build your sensual connection one fingertip at a time.

Mindful Sex: Great Sex Is All in Your Head

What is mindful sex, and why might you want to practice it? Mindful sex involves deliberately bringing focus and curiosity to your sensual life with your partner. After all, mindfulness and making love are both practices of awareness. Sexuality is one of the only experiences where non-meditators may suddenly experience a calm, concentrated state of present-moment happiness, where their thinking mind settles, and they become absorbed in sensation as it unfolds. So, imagine what can happen when you deliberately slow down your usual rush to orgasm and cultivate this sensory awareness during sex, rather than waiting for focus to occur occasionally and accidentally. With mindful sex, you can practice leaving your head behind and becoming one with your breath and your lover's breath, your heart and your lover's heart, your body and your lover's body. Quite simply, mindfulness can make you a better lover, and one who has way more pleasure and fun.

Sex becomes a meditative experience when you deeply inhabit the moment together, and everything outside the current touch, smell, sound, sight, and taste fades away. Mindful sex helps you explore your sensual possibilities and to put the play back into foreplay. A lingering erotic kiss good-bye, a playful smack on the butt as you leave the shower, a teasing text at noon—these mindful moments of lust and love can help you come together in passion at the end of the day. You will learn many mindful sex techniques in the following two chapters. But first, let's look at how you can use mindfulness to turn yourself on.

MINDFUL SKILL: Giving and Receiving Focused Sensual Touch

This practice combines the teachings of mindfulness with the classic sex therapy technique of sensate focus devised by the sex researchers Masters and Johnson. I want you to explore sensual contact without having any goals of sexual arousal or orgasm, by allowing your touching to roam over all of your partner's body except for breasts and genitals. Excluding the more directly erogenous zones and exploring the rest of the body will awaken your sensuality and expand the ways in which touch can create pleasure.

This is a two-part exercise; you will each take turns being the giver of touch and the receiver of touch. In terms of mindfulness practice, take the point of touch contact—between fingertips and the sole of the foot, between tongue and neck—as the meditation object. Focus your attention on the direct experience of the sensations. What does this touch actually feel like?

When your attention wanders into distraction, into planning dinner or listening to traffic noise, catch your mind and gently refocus on the physical sensations at the point of contact.

Begin by deciding who will be the giver first and how long the first half of the touch session will be. I suggest between fifteen and thirty minutes. Set a timer. Get naked. The receiver then lies down on their back and closes their eyes. The giver gently places a hand on their beloved's heart. Together, take three mindful, slow breaths. As the giver, begin to touch your partner anywhere from the top of the head to the tips of the toes, excluding breasts and genitals. Practice in silence, other than softly asking your sweetheart to turn over. Drop your preconceived ideas about how your partner likes to be touched and trace their skin with today's fingertips, here and now, for the very first time. Be curious and explore. Pay attention to the sensation of pressure and pace, warmth and coolness, rough and smooth at your fingertips. Then use your palms, lips, tongue, hair, elbows—be creative. Then switch roles.

When you are being touched by your partner, focus on the direct sensation. Get out of your head and into your body. If you worry that your partner must be bored or that you should feel a certain way about this touch, gently redirect your attention to the touch itself. Practice staying in the present moment without craving sexual arousal or orgasm. Learn what it actually feels like to be touched this way right now. Really notice how each sensation feels. Notice what you find pleasant, what you find neutral, and what you find unpleasant. When does titillate turn into tickle? How does soft, subtle touch compare to direct, intense touch? You may discover new pleasure sensations. Just experience them without clinging and allow them to be replaced naturally when your partner changes to another type of touch.

When you have both completed your mindful touch exploration, settle into an embrace. Lay together, breathing and being, honoring your bodies, your minds, and your hearts.

Desire and Arousal: Starting Your Erotic Engine

Have you ever had an orgasm while meditating? One of my students reports that her meditation sometimes comes with a side dish of "Oh My!" She worries that she's weird, and asked, "Isn't mindfulness about, well, the mind? Why do I get turned on?" I explained that by slowing her mind and focusing deeply on her breath and bodily sensations, she was noticing pleasant sensual or sexual feelings that she was previously unaware of. It's not that meditating was making her horny. Rather, when she quieted her normal background buzz of mental distraction, she contacted physical sensations that she usually ignores. The body can be aroused, but the mind may not be aware of it until we pay attention. That's why both men and women can orgasm in their sleep, without any direct sexual stimulation whatsoever. Once you understand desire and arousal—the mind and body aspects of what happens when you begin to feel turned on—you can increase your sexual appetite using mindfulness.

The way I like to teach couples to understand how to start their erotic engine is by differentiating between desire mind and physical arousal. Sexual desire happens in your head—it includes mental feelings, thoughts, and fantasies of sensual turned-on-ness or horniness. Sexual arousal happens in your body and includes engorgement of the tissues of the penis, clitoris, or labia; lubrication; and other physical signs and sensations. When you begin to feel turned on, you are experiencing either desire or arousal or both. It is a myth that desire and arousal always occur together; your own sexual history tells you that. Sometimes you feel sexually aroused out of the blue—you are cooking an omelet, and you notice a delicious warm throb in your groin and realize you are horny, but your mind is thinking about whether to add truffles to the eggs, not about sex. Alternatively, you turn your mind to an erotic fantasy or you notice how sexy your sweetheart looks as he vacuums up the cat hair, and you experience desire in the mind. The body may not be aroused at all yet, but the mind is. But what does mindfulness have to do with it?

In her book, *Better Sex Through Mindfulness*, Lori Brotto says that paying attention to sensation is a critical aspect of satisfying sexual functioning. Distraction and inattention interfere with healthy sexual arousal for both men and women at both the physical level (blood flow and lubrication) and the psychological level (reported feelings of being turned on). Encouragingly, improving attention with mindfulness practice does seem to boost sexual function and increase concordance between mental desire and physical arousal. In one study conducted in Brotto's lab, as few as three ninety-minute mindfulness sessions significantly improved several aspects of sexual response in women with low sexual desire. There is a growing body of evidence for the impact of mindfulness meditation on happy, healthy sexuality. Says Brotto (2018), "I would argue that satisfying sex is quite simply *not possible* without mindfulness. Acrobatic sex or willful stamina are not what make sex truly magnificent. In my opinion, it is mindfulness." So, you see, there really is a reason to bring Buddha into the bedroom.

But first, you have to want to get to the bedroom. Feeling sexually motivated is a tricky thing, particularly when you have been with one sexual partner for a long time. As you know, occasionally sexual desire or arousal appear without any effort on your part—suddenly you want to rip your sweetie's clothes off and dive between their legs. But over time, spontaneous lust and thrill energy usually fade. Partner familiarity—that is, being in a long-term relationship—predicts low sexual desire and decreased frequency of lovemaking in both sexes. Therefore, most couples cannot rely on spontaneous desire and arousal if they want to have a robust sexual life together. Instead of waiting around for passion, they need to *become* passion. And there are two keys they can use to start their erotic engine and warm it up—the desire key and the arousal key.

Let's say you haven't had sex in a couple of weeks or even months, and you are not feeling at all sexually motivated. You can deliberately cultivate mental desire by first calming your mind and minimizing distracting thoughts. Then use your imagination to turn yourself on—fantasize about a particularly hot encounter you had with your beloved or imagine dripping massage oil on them tonight. Alternatively, you can begin with arousal instead of desire. Even if your mind is busy and worried, you can take a bath and begin to slowly soap your body, caressing yourself and teasing your body into arousal. By paying mindful attention to the physical sensations of sexual arousal, you can tune in and turn on. This is not easy to do: if there were a quick fix for desire and arousal problems, this would be a very short book. But take heart. You can use the focus you cultivate in meditation practice to improve your sexual desire, connect with your sexual arousal, and have more and better sex. You have the keys to your erotic engine. Awakened lovers use the keys often because great couples plan for passion. So, practice cultivating your own desire and arousal, deliberately strengthening the two pathways that lead you into your lover's arms.

MINDFUL SKILL: Cultivate Your Desire with Erotic Imagination

Sit or lie down in a very comfortable position. Adjust your body so it is supported and relaxed. Then gently close your eyes and spend a few moments placing your attention on the breath. Allow your mind to settle down. Place a touch of a smile on your lips. Then recall a time when you made love with your partner, one that was particularly sensual and pleasurable for you. Perhaps it was an occasion where you were particularly frisky, hot, or naughty or the first time you made love when the urgency and novelty were sparkling. Choose a scenario. Next, begin to recall, visualize, and imagine your experience of this sexual encounter. Can you recall how their mouth felt on yours? Can you feel the touch of their fingertips running over your body? As with any mindfulness practice, if your mind wanders and you start thinking about something else, redirect your attention to the meditation object—the erotic memory. Deepen your experience of the mental lovemaking, paying attention to all of your senses—imagining the scent of their shampoo, the sound of their moans, the sight of their nude back, the taste of their mouth, and the increasing pleasure of the touch between you. Bring to mind as much detail as you can. Then make the memory even hotter. Imagine the urgency of your bodies as you approach orgasm, the flood of pleasure, the release, the joy. Turn yourself on in your mind by thinking about sex with your beloved. And when you are ready to end the exercise, open your eyes.

Practice this meditation often. And not just lying down—play with erotic memories on your drive home from work. Cultivating mental desire is a profound practice, one that can increase your sexual arousal and the frequency of your lovemaking. Once you create mental desire, you can choose to connect with your partner sexually tonight, rather than just waiting for it to happen. No matter how tired your body is, you can ignite a spark of passion in your head. So, explore desire mind, and enjoy.

LOVE SKILL: Cultivate Your Arousal with Solo Sensual Touch

No matter how distracted your mind is, you can ignite a spark of passion in your body by touching yourself until you are aroused. This is not a simple masturbation exercise. For one thing, you stop before orgasm, and for another, you touch yourself in new ways to explore new sensations all over your body. Once your body is turned on, your mind can catch up and be willing to play. Then it's time to take your beloved to bed.

Lie down, naked, in a comfortable position. You may want to practice this meditation in bed or in the bathtub and to have massage oil or a water-based lubricant available for the body and genital touching. Begin by focusing on your breath for a few moments. Then, gently scan your body with your mind and notice how the body feels in various places. What does the pressure of the bed or bath feel like under your heels, your buttocks, your head? Where do you feel warmth or coolness? Next, begin to gently trail your fingertips along your body. Start by stroking your hands and arms. Notice the sensations. Notice what the mind is doing—what emotions or thoughts or stories are present? Invite the mind to stop chasing these distractions and instead focus on the sensation of fingertips on skin. Don't worry if the mind won't cooperate. Just continue exploring touch. Move your hands over your body in whatever direction and in whatever manner feels good. Linger on any areas that feel pleasurable, erotic, or arousing. Eventually begin touching your most sexually sensitive areas—perhaps your breasts, nipples, penis, clitoris, vagina. Bring your awareness to your genitals. Experience the sensations as you turn yourself on and arouse your sexual pleasure. Be curious and touch yourself in new ways; don't follow your typical self-pleasure routine. Explore new forms of erotic touch. If you usually stroke your clitoris gently, try using more pressure, touching your labia, or sliding a finger inside your vagina and contracting your muscles. Or if you usually slide your hand on the lower shaft of your penis, try playing with the tip or caressing your testicles. If the mind wants to escape into sexual fantasy, bring it back—pay attention to the direct sensations of physical touch and sexual arousal as they are occurring right here and now. If the mind "needs" something to do, silently describe the sensations to yourself, *It feels good when I rub myself here.... I'm touching my clit and feeling turned on.*

After you have practiced mindful sensual touch for a period of time, gradually stop all movement. If you are in a heightened state of sexual arousal, notice what that feels like in stillness. What sensations are still there? Notice where and how you feel arousal—perhaps a tingling in the clitoris and a pleasant achy feeling in the lower abdomen or a strong pleasure in the penis and a relaxed pleasant warmth in the lower back. You will likely uncover aspects of your arousal that you were previously unaware of. Be curious. Discover more about how it feels when you are sexually turned on. Enjoy it, here and now, without grasping for an orgasm. Then let all the exploration go and lie still, simply attending to breathing in and breathing out. Gently wiggle your fingers and toes. Feel your entire body. When you are ready, open your eyes. And then go jump your partner.

Visit http://www.drcherylfraser.com/buddhasbedroom for additional teaching on arousal and desire.

Sexual Desire Disconnect: I Want Sex, You Don't

"I could have sex twice a day," Anna says. Raj looks crestfallen as his wife continues, "I want him to initiate sex, and I want more frequent sex. It feels like he isn't attracted to me." The biggest complaint couples bring to a sex therapist's office is, "I want to have sex more often than my partner." Raj and Anna are a fairly typical example of sexual desire disconnect. Their love affair began with great romance and passion. They were very attracted to each other, made love every other day, tried new sexual positions and toys, and attended the occasional fetish party dressed up in sexy leather costumes. Their sex life was, according to both of them, great. But over time, as lust and novelty faded, when Raj became the head of his division and his work pressures mounted, and after they had their daughter, their sex life slowly changed. They had sex less often, then the sex became routine, and then they stopped most creative sensual delights—toys, games, sexy parties. But Anna's level of desire for sex and her ease of sexual arousal remained quite high. At first, she kept her hurt and disappointment silent. Then she started to ask for sex more often or to encourage Raj to tell her a fantasy he's like to act out. She set up schedules so they would have sex three times a week.

She even bought Raj a new sex toy for Father's Day in the hopes she could reignite passion. But instead of turning Raj on, her requests, demands, and eventual complaints turned him off. "I feel like I'm a failure as a lover. And frankly, I am so tired and stressed that I just don't want to have sex very often. I think Anna is beautiful, and it's not like I want to sleep with anyone else—I'm just not that into sex anymore."

I reminded Raj and Anna that it's normal for sexual passion to fade over time, and that they need to make their sex life a hobby. I encouraged Raj to practice turning his mind toward sex, instead of away from it. He agreed to stop checking work emails after 7:00 p.m., and then to take a long steam shower and relax while he deliberately cultivates desire mind. He proposed that Anna join him in the shower ten minutes later so he's had that alone time to begin to calm his mind and ground into his body. Once Anna steps in, he asked that she embrace him, and they connect their bodies and hearts with a naked three-breath hug. Then, depending on his needs, sometimes he chooses to soap her body, enjoying the sensuality of her slippery skin, and he is able to gradually become sexually aroused. "But sometimes I just can't get my head in the game—I am chewing on a work problem and even my gorgeous wife is not enough to wake my sexuality up." Anna chimes in, "I love being naked in the shower with you, and I am usually pretty horny by then ... if you are having trouble getting out of your head, I am happy to go down on you, and I bet that'll help!" Anna's playful, relaxed attitude toward sex is something Raj always loved, so he laughs and says, "Well, gee, you are offering me a blow job to help me get in the mood? Sounds good to me!"

I call this "desire bypass"—when one partner has no sexual desire, I ask the partner who does to dive in and create sexual arousal in their sweetie, giving caresses, kisses, massage, or oral sex, turning their partner on until they are ready to make love. Desire mind can then catch up during the sex itself. A common example is a heterosexual couple where the man wakes up with an erection and would love to have morning sex, but the woman awakes groggy and with no desire or arousal whatsoever. I suggest that in that case the man offer to give his sweetie oral sex as her mind and body gradually wake up. Once she's aroused, they have a quickie, and then leave bed mutually satisfied, sipping coffee with smiling faces and relaxed, happy bodies.

If you have sexual desire differences, rest assured you are not broken. Researcher Rosemary Basson, in her model of the female circular sexual response cycle, suggests that beginning a sexual encounter from a place of sexual neutrality—no apparent desire or arousal—is quite normal in long-term couples, particularly for women. Her model supports the desire bypass approach I use—if you are not in the mood, ask your sweetie to start your erotic engine with the arousal key and simply bypass mental desire. It can appear later, once the car is already moving along lovers' lane. This is a very important teaching: *sexual desire does not need to be present before you start a sexual encounter.* You can create it during your festivities.

So how might this play out in your relationship? One method is to work on your own level of desire or arousal, taking the time to get turned on, and then approaching your sweetie. The other is to ask your partner to turn you on—you start touching and kissing even if you are not inspired, and in time, your desire and arousal emerge. The good news is that sexual desire disconnect does not have to dictate whether or not you have sex. Make sensuality a priority. By working with your mind as well as your body, you can find ways, together, to have a richer, more frequent, and passionate sexual life.

LOVE SKILL: Never Say "I'm Not in the Mood" Ever Again

Picture the following scenario. You're in the kitchen preparing lunch. You're worried because you really need to finish that last little bit of your tax return. Your sweetheart comes into the kitchen in an amorous mood, slides their hands around your waist from behind, kisses your neck, and says, "I've got a half hour; you want to go to bed?" Freeze-frame right there. Now, that is a sexy, sweet, wonderful invitation. But what happens next? You say, "I'm not in the mood," and shrug your partner away. And just like that, a connection is broken, and a possibility is ended. Now, to be fair to you, you are not in the mood for sex! Taxes don't make you horny. You are simply not connected with your desire or arousal. For many couples, refusing sex has become the automatic response to an amorous pass. But it doesn't have to be. When one of you wants sex and the other doesn't, remember that desire and arousal are choices. Whether you are currently tuned on or not, you can take a pause, apply mindfulness, and allow your head to get you into bed. Sexual arousal is a multifaceted thing. Just because you're not turned on right now doesn't mean you can't warm up in a short while. So here is the instruction I give to my clients who rarely get naked together. Practice this diligently for the next month, and then for the rest of your lives: *never say "I'm not in the mood" ever again.*

I don't mean the partner who doesn't feel aroused should just "give in and have sex." I am simply reminding you that getting "in the mood" may not be as difficult as you think, particularly if you know how to meditate. When you give a flat "no" to a sex request, you slam the door on sensuality without even giving yourself a chance to spark arousal or desire. What might happen if instead of saying no, you take a moment for a breath, then lean back into those embracing arms, and say, "Hmm, give me a few minutes, honey," or "Not right now, but ask me after lunch." That's not a rejection, it's a possibility. You create a gap to cultivate your desire or your arousal (or both). Slow down your thinking. Relax with some deep breathing and focus on opening your heart. Turn your attention toward the erotic. Imagine how fun it will be to make love. Connect with your body and sexy feelings. Then go find your partner. Kiss them, mindfully. Take your time. There is nowhere else to be, nothing else to do. Just the two of you, here and now, enjoying one caress at a time. Take your sweetie to bed. Trust that even if your sexual interest is low as you begin connecting sexually, it can ignite during the process. Sometimes you need to idle for a while before your erotic engine is ready to engage.

Role-play this with your partner because it takes practice to change a habit. Approach your mate and say, "Hey, so do you want to make love?" or "I'm kind of frisky," or whatever you might say or do to initiate lovemaking. Then your partner will role-play rejecting you by saying, "I'm not in the mood." Have a giggle. Then do it again, but this time when you initiate, your partner will say, "Not right now, honey, but ask me later," or something similar. Then switch roles—your partner asks, and you reject. Then they ask again, and this time you say maybe. Pay attention to how it feels to be turned down and how it feels when the possibility for sensual connection is kept alive.

Love Bytes

♥ Mindfulness can make you a way better lover—present, connected, sensually alive, and playful.

♥ Your erotic engine has two keys. Sexual desire happens in the mind; sexual arousal happens in the body.

♥ The problem? They want sex, and you don't. The solution? Never say, "I'm not in the mood" ever again.

♥ Practice desire bypass: if desire or arousal is not yet present, begin making love anyway and let pleasure unfold.

Buddha Bytes

❧ Sex and meditation have a lot to do with each other. In fact, great sex is all in your head.

❧ Awakened lovers slow their mind, show up in their body, and experience pleasure with presence.

❧ Learn to give and receive sensual touch without any goals of arousal or orgasm, and discover new ways to connect.

❧ Mindful loving asks you to let go of expectations and allow your sensuality the space and time to awaken.

CHAPTER 10

Loving Effort
Seven Steps to Enlightened Sex

If the Buddha were your lover, what would the sex be like? Imagine that you approach your beloved with curiosity and focus. You are able to pay full attention to every sensation in your own body and theirs. You explore connection in every possible way, using mind, body, and words, and you cultivate passion and joy. You see things as they really are and let go of expectations so you can deeply appreciate this moment, this touch, as it is right now, wanting nothing other. Your mind and body become one and melt with the mind and body of your partner, surrendering, merging, experiencing rapture and wonder. Your heart is fully open, and your whole being is awakened love. You share bliss and sexual ecstasy and experience freedom from all suffering. Orgasm is a taste of enlightenment. That's what it might be like if you made love with the Buddha. And that's what it can feel like when you make love with your sweetheart tonight—if you make loving effort, cultivating the seven qualities of enlightened mind and applying them to enlightened sex.

I'll bet you are interested in having transcendent sex with your beloved. And you can. But it does take effort to become enlightened, after all. Same with enlightened sex. It turns out we don't just fall off a meditation cushion and become a fully awake, passionate lover. It takes practice. The Buddha taught that there are seven factors of enlightenment, and our old friend *mindfulness* is the first quality. The other factors are *curiosity, enthusiasm, bliss, tranquility, concentration,* and *equanimity*. You already have these capacities within your mind; they just need to be uncovered and developed. As a child watching an anthill, you were curious, focused, energized, and filled with pleasure. There was nowhere you'd rather be. Meditation helps you access and nourish these inherent positive mind qualities. These same qualities of mind, when applied to love and sex, can help awaken the lover that lives inside you.

But what would this actually feel like off the cushion, on an average day with your partner? Imagine relaxing with your mate and noticing that all the seven factors of awakening are present. Your mind is peaceful and refreshed. You are not worrying about the past or the future—your mundane concerns have receded, and you are mindful and aware of this moment with your sweetheart. You feel tranquil and focused as your beloved strokes your palm with their fingertip, and you fully experience the sensual pleasure and mental bliss of the touch and the moment. You concentrate on the sensation with curiosity, and you feel a sense of enthusiasm and vitality as you begin to caress their hand, focusing on their skin, their breath, how they respond to your touch. There is energy in the interest and a simple sense of happiness and equanimity—the disagreement you had with your mate this morning is now viewed with a broad and loving perspective, and you accept this moment, and your mate, just as they are right now. You nibble their lower lip. Arousal and desire arise, and the kisses and caresses intensify. You are connecting, body and mind, as awakened lovers.

Each of the following sections in this chapter takes one of the seven factors of enlightenment, from mindfulness to equanimity, and applies it to your sexual life. Train your head and bring it into bed. That is the path to enlightened sex, to bringing Buddha into the bedroom.

1. Mindfulness: Too Much of a Good Thing?

Brenna and Salim have been together for fifteen years. "We actually met at a meditation retreat," Brenna laughs. They've come to me for help with their sexual life. "We both meditate regularly, and we have a very calm, sweet relationship, but the spark is just not there." As I get more history from this couple, it becomes clear to me that they are, in a manner of speaking, too mindful. Mindfulness is probably the most important key to being an awakened lover, but mindfulness is only one of the seven factors of awakening. Sometimes, an overreliance on the practice of mindfulness leads to a flat meditation, where the mind is not joyful or enlivened. The meditator becomes an aloof observer and forgets to enjoy the experience. Salim shares the following, "We made love this weekend, and it was okay. I was really focusing on the sensations of touch and noticing my breathing changing as I neared orgasm. But there was no passion ... I actually felt a bit disconnected, sort of like a robotic feeling of going through the motions. I wasn't thinking about other things—meditation has really helped calm my mind—but it was a bit blah."

The awake mind feels beautiful, not blah. So should the awake bedroom. In passion triangle terms, Brenna and Salim have superior intimacy skills, but they lack the thrill and sensuality of mindful loving. This couple has inadvertently made meditation—and lovemaking—too much of a head trip. They need to enliven their mindfulness, get out of their heads and into their bodies, and awaken lust, joy, and playfulness. They need to bring more fun and energy to their meditation and to their love life. I can see that they need to cultivate the other factors of enlightenment, with particular emphasis on the three active, pleasurable qualities of mind and of enlightened sex: curiosity, enthusiasm, and bliss. As a test, I ask Salim to reach out and stroke Brenna's arm. I watch him concentrate, brow furrowed. I ask him to narrate what he is experiencing. "Her skin is warm. I feel the different textures. I experience the movement of my finger, the tightening of the tiny muscles." Then I ask him how sexy it feels, and he bursts into an embarrassed grin. "Um, not at all?" "Exactly!" I exclaim. "You've 'mindfulled' all the fun, joy, and horniness out of that touch—no wonder sex feels robotic. You need to put the play back in foreplay and the fullness back in mindfulness."

I suggest that, over the next month, Brenna and Salim explore connecting mindfulness with passion. I know that if they develop the other factors of enlightened mind and enlightened sex, stroking an arm will become an extraordinary erotic experience. So, if you, like Brenna and Salim, have lost the play and joy of sex, let's look at how you can bring them back. Let's wake up your mindfulness with a little help from its friends, the six other enlightenment factors.

2. Curiosity: No More "Nipple Nipple Crotch Good-Night"

When was the last time you licked the back of your partner's knees, or danced naked to a sensual beat, or had wild sex up against the living room wall? Our sex lives often collapse into a repetitive pattern I call "nipple nipple crotch good-night." And you know what I mean. If you are like the majority of long-term couples, your sex life has become infrequent and predictable. The average sexual encounter lasts an astonishingly quick seven minutes—and that is from nudge, wink, to snore. Yikes. You used to make love for hours—or at least for longer than seven minutes—with curiosity and enthusiasm, exploring sweet gentle lovemaking, hot raw sex, and everything in between. But these days, chances are you've forgotten to make your sex life a priority. You've become bored with the familiar. So, it's time to practice the second factor of enlightened sex: curiosity.

The Buddha taught us to have a curious, investigative mind. Brenna and Salim arrived in my office because they are curious about their lack of sexual passion, curious how they can ignite it, and curious how their mindful life can also be a passionate one. You are reading this book for the same reasons. Imagine that you are in the world's largest paint store, and there are thousands upon thousands of colors available to you. Would you limit your palette to blue and green? No. So stop doing that with your sensual life. Your body starts at the soles of your feet and extends to the crown of your head, and there are endless possibilities to connect through the five senses, from feeling the butterfly kiss of flickering eyelashes on cheek to hearing moans of ecstasy to watching your partner pleasure themselves to tasting their salty skin to scenting their musk. Start exploring the entire glorious palette of sensuality.

And enlightened sex is not just about sweetness and light. I encourage couples to open up to what I call *dark sensual energy* as well. This is the lusty, the raw, the primal part of your sexuality. You may feel some confusion or even shame about these aspects of your arousal and curiosity. Perhaps you desire to be tied up and treated like a sex slave, or you fantasize about having an orgy, or picking up a stranger on an airplane and rutting in the tiny bathroom stall. You may cut off that part of your sensuality, or compartmentalize it away from your lovemaking, never sharing your dark energy urges with your beloved. As awakened lovers, we think of ourselves as conscious, sophisticated beings with a spiritual path. We are ethical, generous, kind, and compassionate. And nice. Really nice. But we also have deep, powerful sexual energy, a vital libido or life-force. And this dark sensual energy wants to play dirty, not nice.

Enlightened sex does not always have to be so darn nice and polite. Sure, sometimes you slowly, sweetly make love together and weep with the depth of loving, intimate connection, but sometimes you want to unleash the raw power of the complementary dark energy of passion and joyfully fuck and be fucked by the one you love. These are both wonderful aspects of the palette of sensuality. Too often people turn away from their deepest lusty sexual energy because they label it as bad. In Buddhism, things are not good or bad. They are skillful or unskillful, depending on whether they cause suffering or lead away from suffering. In fact, dark sensual energy only leads to suffering when it is cut off or when it leaks out in unwholesome ways. When you deny the truth of your powerful dark sexual energy, you are disconnecting your groin from your head and your heart. That is not mindful loving; that is repression.

Liberating and playing with your dark sexual energy with your partner can be a beautiful and meaningful part of your sexual connection. You can combine deep trust and intimacy with the thrill of the taboo and the rawness of sexual sensuality. Can you bring curiosity and mindful acceptance to the parts of your sexual desire and longing that you may have been ignoring? By doing so, you can begin to connect groin, heart, and head and play with myriad colors of sensuality. You can liberate some aspects of passion and presence that you have been compartmentalizing. So, stop limiting yourself to "nipple nipple crotch good-night" or ho-hum nice sex. Bye-bye, sensual rut; hello, creativity. Get curious about what turns you on, and which colors of the sensual palette you'd like to paint your lover with—both dark and light.

MINDFUL SKILL: Expand Your Sensual Repertoire

It is time to get curious, explore, and expand your personal sensual repertoire. But before you attempt to get creative in bed, think about what turns you on and what might turn you on. I invite you to contemplate the following questions.

First, ask yourself, What turns me on? You can interpret this question in whatever way works for you personally. Perhaps you are turned on by a romantic scenario, soft music, murmured sweet nothings. Or you love to see your partner naked. Or you like to talk dirty or dress in leather chaps. Nothing is off-limits here because what turns you on is a personal part of your eroticism. It may have been a long time since you got curious about your personal turn-ons. So, spend some time—and have some fun—making a list of things that ignite your passion.

Second, ask, What sexual activities would I like to try? Perhaps you'd like to try anal sex, or you'd like to role-play that you are strangers who meet on the beach one night and have urgent, thrilling sex under the stars. (PS: Take a blanket. Sand in your bliss points is not erotic.) Once you have your lists of what turns you on and what you'd like to explore, share them with your partner. Listen curiously and notice which of your partner's ideas spark interest, desire, or arousal in you. Then choose one idea from each list that you will explore this month.

Third, I invite you to revisit the passion plan you began in chapter 8. But this time, really focus on the sensuality side of your passion triangle. Commit to some daily and weekly erotic activities. Perhaps commit to kissing passionately every day. Maybe you'll schedule sex twice a week and commit to making love on those days no matter what, because as you've learned, you don't need to be in the mood to decide to get into the mood. And don't forget to incorporate some of your turn-ons and things you want to try. Then print a copy of your master passion plan and post it in your bedroom.

Visit http://www.drcherylfraser.com/buddhasbedroom to watch a video teaching on your passion plan with bonus material.

LOVE SKILL: Playing with Dark Sensual Energy

Awakened lovers connect dark sensual energy with love, vulnerability, and trust. In fact, unleashing some of the raw, intense, primal aspects of your sexuality is a very powerful type of passion—one that combines thrill, intimacy, and sensuality. Dark sensual energy contains tremendous power—power that can be harnessed and utilized for deep connection, bliss, and enlightenment. But first, you need to liberate this libido, or life-force. You can begin by exploring where you are open and where you are closed, where you feel comfortable and where you feel awkward or embarrassed. Can you play with the light and the dark and ground your lust in love? You've built a foundation of thrill, intimacy, communication, and nonjudgment. You've built a safe, connected playground within which to explore your dark sexual energy, together. Here are a few suggestions to get you started. (Note that I am inviting you to move out of your comfort zone, but I am not asking you to move out of your safety zone. Each person and each couple will discern what they are willing to explore and where they need to say, "I am not interested in exploring that at this time.")

♥ Create a detailed erotic fantasy about a taboo that turns you on, something that feels arousing and intriguing but also, perhaps, a bit uncomfortable. This fantasy should feature you and your beloved doing something hot. It should be a desire that you have never shared with them. Now to be clear—fantasy is just that. You may or may not wish to act this fantasy out. But I do want you to describe it to your partner in detail. You can write it out in an erotic letter, you can whisper it to them as you cuddle in the dark, and of course, if you are both intrigued and willing, you can indeed take it into action, together.

♥ Take turns being in command of a sexual encounter. The person in control gets to dictate what they want, to tell their sweetheart what to do, and when and how they do it. Play with power and play with the delight of surrender. When you are in the role of surrender, notice how liberating it can feel to have no responsibility—or guilt—about unleashing your sexual lust, simply because you've agreed to trust your partner and to do what they direct. When you are in the role of sensual control, notice how it feels to ask for whatever you want without shame.

♥ Talk dirty to me, baby. Give voice to your lust as well as your love. Play with making sounds when you have sex. Raise the roof with moans and squeals of delight. What happens if you talk dirty during sex? Do you feel embarrassed but also aroused? Many couples find this challenging—they roll around in sweaty delight but do so silently. Discover what it feels like to be vocal during sex, and in addition to whispering sweet nothings, try shouting salty somethings. And when you are not naked, use your words to titillate, to seduce, to turn each other on. In addition to love notes or texts, send lust notes. "I can't wait to feel your wetness tonight." "You were so hot in bed last night—I love it when you let go and just fuck me."

3. Enthusiasm: Make Sex Your Hobby

When I next meet with Brenna and Salim, they update me on their curiosity explorations. "It's been interesting, to say the least!" says Brenna. "For me, it was very powerful to examine what turns me on. I realized I didn't really know. I mean, I like kissing. I like how orgasm feels, but I guess I'd never really allowed myself to be curious about my deep sexual desires." I ask her how it was to share her turn-ons with her husband. "It was surprisingly vulnerable. I told him I have a recurring fantasy where I am having sex with my college boyfriend in the chemistry lab, and I see the professor at the door, watching us. He unzips his pants and plays with his erection. Now, this never really happened, but I love to fantasize I'm being watched by one man while another man makes me come. Salim says he was intrigued and turned on by my fantasy, and we definitely had more, and more varied, sex for a while. But now we are back to almost none." I compliment them for making loving effort and for bringing curiosity to their love life. "You had some great results, but to sustain the sensual exploration, you need to cultivate more enthusiasm or energy—the next factor of enlightened sex," I advise. "Curiosity introduces you to what is possible, and energy helps you make it happen."

According to the Buddha's teaching, the mental quality of enthusiasm, also translated as "energy" or "vitality," is, well, vital if you want to reach enlightenment. This quality is experienced as a zest, a life-force, a sense of thrill. Energy sparks enthusiasm and helps us persevere in meditation and in love, to make the necessary effort to create what we want. I advise Brenna and Salim to direct their energy toward planning elaborate or erotic sex dates. They protest that planning sex isn't romantic, and I counter with, "You know what's not romantic? Having boring sex." I point out that by planning something special, they can create erotic anticipation, turn on their desire, and keep the flow of erotic energy moving. By investing in passion and making their sex life a hobby, they can renew enthusiasm and keep sex fresh and exciting.

LOVE SKILL: Plan for Passion with Sexual IOUs

Plan an elaborate sexual encounter once a month—where you explore one of your not-yet-tried turn-ons—as an exciting way to spice up your sensual life. To make this even more fun and creative and to build anticipation, I suggest you create sensual IOUs. These are promises for a sexy, passionate date. For example:

- ♥ I owe you an entire day off from all housework and childcare. I'll take the kids to my mom's house while you have a long candlelit bath and sip champagne. When I get home, I will give you a sensual massage and then feed you chocolate mousse in bed. Then I'll tie you up, lick chocolate off your body, and give you the most erotic night of oral sex you've experienced—making you come again and again.

- ♥ I owe you a night where I will meet you at the bar of the fancy hotel downtown. I'll be dressed up, looking sexy, and I ask you to do the same. Don't wear underwear because I'm going to flirt with you over dinner and play with you under the table. Then I'm taking you dancing and after to a romantic room upstairs for hot sex.

I want you and your partner to each create six IOUs and exchange them. Then take turns cashing in one IOU on alternate months—which gives you lots of time to anticipate and fantasize. Or, if you love the element of surprise, exchange your IOUs in sealed envelopes and open them one at a time—flip a coin to decide who goes first this month—the winner chooses one of the envelopes they received from their spouse and opens it. Then plan and participate in that sexy date with all the curiosity, enthusiasm, and unbridled sensuality you can uncover.

4. Bliss: Explore Pleasure and Joy

What a simple thing, pleasure. And yet, all too often we have relapsed from the relationship pleasure we used to revel in and are taking refuge in Marriage Inc. Instead of seeking to give and receive pleasure together, we run from obligation to obligation and fall into bed exhausted. If we have sex, it's the "nipple nipple crotch goodnight" routine once again. Well, it's time to bring pleasure, in all its forms, back.

The fourth factor of enlightenment is bliss, pleasure, rapture, or joy. In meditation, as the mind gets curious about the object—breath—this pleasurable focus generates energy, which helps the mind collect itself, concentrate, and calm down. The enlightenment factors work together, and a sense of bliss wells up. The mind is joyful and bright, and tingling pleasure moves through the body. Yes, this feels fantastic, with flavors ranging from gently yummy to ecstasy—so much so that some folks get addicted to these blissful meditation states. And yes, you can make love like this—providing you train your mind and make some loving effort in your relationship. Take the time to slow down and indulge in the small and large raptures of your sensual body. Cultivate a joyfulness in your sexual life. Remember how to turn foreplay into for-play. If you are like many couples, you likely need to lighten up and have more fun. Blast the music from your teenage years and dance around the kitchen together. Laugh more. Touch more. Life is pretty serious sometimes, and dukkha is real. So, it's vital to notice all the moments of sun beneath the clouds and unleash the beauty, joy, and bliss of this very moment. Perhaps with chocolate body paint.

MINDFUL SKILL: Cultivate Sexual Pleasure with Mutual Erotic Touch

It is time to explore mutual touch between you and your partner that includes the whole body and moves into lovemaking and orgasm, if you wish it to.

Begin by embracing, naked and face-to-face, either lying on your side or with one of you lying on top of the other. Start tuning in to the physical sensations, focusing on the points where your bodies are touching. Take a few breaths together and experience the sensations of your chests moving together. The practice of mutual touch means you give and receive at the same time, in an overlapping erotic dance, so both of you get to experiment with shifting the focus of attention back and forth from the pleasurable sensations of touching and being touched. The purpose of this exercise is to make pleasure the focus of the experience. If it feels good, do it. Slowly start touching each other. You may stroke your partner's skin or kiss them deeply. Notice the sensations and warmth of your fingertips stroking their body, of their tongue on yours. By slowing down your usual pace and breaking up your typical routine, you can begin to notice the plethora of pleasurable sensations. Move your focus from one bliss point to another as you begin to caress each other's chest, legs, anywhere on the body. Sometimes you may take turns and give and receive, then return to mutual touch. You are making love with mindfulness.

In time, you will move to genital touching and focus on the sensation of your sexual arousal. But instead of narrowing your focus, experiment with trying to hold both your felt pleasure and the sensations of touching your sweetheart in your awareness at the same time. You are making love with, not being made love to. Can you find the subtle pleasures in sliding your finger up and down their thigh—the tingle in your fingertip—as well as the obvious pleasure of them touching your thigh in a manner you experience as wildly erotic? Can you discover the gently yummy as well as the ecstatic? Then, focus on the pleasure of penetration. (Both opposite sex and same sex couples can explore this—penetrating vaginally or anally with penis, sex toy, or finger.) After initial penetration, lie together in exquisite stillness, without thrusting. What pleasurable sensations can you discover in contact without movement or expectation? Then slowly begin moving. What does slow feel like, as the giver and as the receiver both, and what does fast feel like? Experience the multitude of sensations in this very moment—the richness of your sensuality. Find the pleasure. Allow the familiar "way we usually have sex" to become new and blissful. And if you choose to orgasm, whether with penetration, oral or manual caresses, or a toy, be as present as possible with the pleasure sensations. Slow down, enjoy, revel in rapture.

5. Tranquility: Make Sex Anticlimactic

"We have sex a lot, but there is no connection," says Claire. Jamie blows out a frustrated sigh. This couple has a frequent and acrobatic sex life, but Claire rarely reaches orgasm during their "hot sex," and she feels emotionally unfulfilled by their fifty shades of sensual variety. They are trying too hard to reach a goal—be that mutual orgasm or the emotional and physical intensity of public sex—but they are missing the exquisite pleasure and peace of the subtle states of mind, body, and heart. Their passion is unbalanced—when they are naked, it's all sensuality and thrill, and little to no intimacy. Instead of striving, they need to relax.

The fifth awakening factor is tranquility, relaxation, or serenity. In meditation, this refers to a mind that is free from mental disquiet, a mind that is at peace. The seven factors work together and support each other. Tranquility balances excitement and grounds enthusiasm. This in turn supports deep concentration, the next factor of enlightened sex. When you deliberately take a breath to calm your body and mind, you are practicing tranquility and improving your mindfulness. In sex, I think of tranquility as the ability to let go of grasping and to rest in the contentment of the experience. I point out to Jamie and Claire that a lot of sexual pleasure is in the letting go—physiologically, muscles need to relax so they can release into the spasms of orgasm. When they chase pleasure, they create agitation instead of flow, and this interferes with Claire's orgasm. When they cling to a future outcome, they are by definition not fully enjoying the current experience. I suggest they explore the more relaxed, calming aspects of sensual connection. Instead of seeking pleasure from novel situations, I ask them to rediscover the eroticism of the mundane—sensual massage or slow, deep kisses. Rather than holding on for the big explosion, I want them to release expectation and focus on the bliss in the simplicity of a touch and to balance their lust with intimacy and peacefulness.

MINDFUL SKILL: Post-Orgasm Awareness Meditation

One excellent way to experience tranquility as it appears naturally in your sexual life is to bring an open, relaxed awareness to your experience post-orgasm. The next time you make love with your partner, after orgasm, move into a comfortable, supportive embrace. One of you may rest your head on the chest of the other, or you can entwine face-to-face or spoon. Create as much body contact as you can. Then allow your awareness to settle. Don't apply effort—this is not a focusing meditation—rather, rest your mind and body in the fullness of the present experience, in the complexity of the many sensations and emotions. Allow your awareness to be open and gentle and diffuse. You can explore experiencing the sensations in your body and mind as a whole, or you may wish to slowly allow your awareness to be pulled from one sensation to another as you melt into tranquility. Perhaps you become aware of the movement of your own or your beloved's heartbeat, or the mood of emotional bliss, or the tingling of the skin on your back. Notice how sensations arise, create an experience, and then pass away. Notice if you feel any urge to chase a pleasurable sensation, to move toward excitation and arousal again, and then notice what it feels like to let go of chasing and rest in the now. Observe what your body and mind feel like post-arousal, as your system settles back into tranquility after excitement. Relax your mind and enjoy.

6. Concentration: Reality Beats Fantasy, So Be Here Now

What do you think about when you are making love? Many people report that they fantasize when they are having sex with their partner. This is the antithesis of mindfulness—instead of being here, now, with you, directly experiencing this touch and moment, I am off in my head, lost in the distraction of making love with someone else somewhere else. This is where the enlightenment factor of concentration comes in. In meditation, concentration is the ability to focus on the chosen object and to allow distractions to settle out, which then helps the mind become unified around whatever we are focusing on. When the mind becomes more tranquil, it can focus in a single-pointed way. This can be a doorway to deep, blissful meditation states and to the experience of the self dissolving. In lovemaking, concentration is the prerequisite for tantric sexuality, which we will talk about in the next chapter on loving concentration.

Therefore, if you want transcendent sex with your partner, you need to concentrate on what is actually occurring and let go of sexual fantasy when you are making love. Yes, sexual fantasy can help spark your desire and arousal, and it can enhance your sexual repertoire. But as a preparation for enlightened sex, I suggest you limit fantasy to your solo sexual life. If you rely on fantasy during partnered sex, it will pull you away from your direct experience of the erotic exchange between you. Think about it—if you are eating a delicious chocolate mousse but fantasizing about apple torte, you are not going to have a complete experience of either chocolate or apple. So, fantasizing about someone else during sex will disconnect you from your partner and the interrelated flow between you, and arguably make your sexual pleasure less pleasurable. If you use fantasy to reach orgasm, you are swooning into an experience other than this. What happens if you drop fantasy, open your eyes, and see the person you love, the one you are making love with? When you make love with your partner, begin to cultivate deep concentration and the ability to be here now.

7. Equanimity: Good Enough Sex Is Great

If you are seeking spectacular, transcendent sexual bliss, you will often be disappointed. Don't blame me; blame the Buddha. In the four facts of life chapter, you learned that wanting something other than what is present leads to suffering. Peace and happiness lie in accepting reality, so dropping expectations greatly increases satisfaction, whether in your mind or in your sexual life. The seventh enlightenment factor, equanimity, is a beautiful quality of mind and heart that emerges when wanting and aversion fall away, and you rest in what is. Equanimity is an inward balance. Things feel "just right, just as they are" and the mind is poised, relaxed, and comfortable. And it feels great; it's a sublime and very satisfying emotional state, where you want nothing other than what is here right now. If mindfulness is nonjudgmental acceptance of whatever is occurring, equanimity is the emotional and cognitive aspect of mindfulness— the gracious acceptance of the here-and-now experience you are being mindful of. Imagine you are snuggled naked with your sweetheart, and you want to make love, so you start caressing their thigh. What would happen if you dropped the expectation of how the sensual touch should evolve and simply touched, with equanimity? You'd be open, curious, energized, focused, and calm, naturally experiencing the factors of enlightenment. You'd experience no longing or disappointment. This would allow you to have pleasure no matter where things end up, in a shag or a snooze.

Interestingly, Buddhism meets sex therapy here in the factor of equanimity. The "good enough sex" model presented by sex therapists Barry McCarthy and Michael Metz discourages a performance-based approach to sex—the mind-set that "sex is only worthwhile if we both orgasm," for example—in favor of a pleasure- and connection-based, exploratory sexuality for couples. Satisfying sexuality is seen as multidimensional, and the definition of what it means to "have sex" is expanded. The focus is on enjoying intimacy and pleasure in an environment of "mutual acceptance." This model compliments mindfulness, as couples are encouraged to show up together for their erotic life, willing and ready to explore without specific goals. The quality of sex—from mediocre to spectacular—is not seen as the point of sensual exploration. The exploration itself is what matters, and couples are encouraged to appreciate good enough sex. That is a beautiful description of equanimity.

So, although it may sound contradictory, if you want great sex, stop seeking great sex. Don't worry about how you want this sexual encounter to go or compare it to the sex you've had before. Make love with equanimity, have sex beyond expectations, and enjoy what is.

Love Bytes

♥ Bring curiosity to lovemaking. Explore the palette of sensuality. No more "nipple nipple crotch good-night."

♥ Dark sensual energy is a beautiful, powerful part of your sensual life. Explore your taboos together.

♥ Scheduled sex is romantic. Plan for passion with sexual IOUs and revel in your sensual hobby.

♥ Reality beats fantasy. So be here now, with this lover, with this breath, in direct experience.

Buddha Bytes

☸ The seven factors of enlightened sex are mindfulness, curiosity, enthusiasm, bliss, tranquility, concentration, and equanimity.

☸ Cultivate more pleasure, bliss, and joy. Put the play back in foreplay.

☸ What do you do after orgasm? Practice awareness of tranquilly and connection and savor the calm that follows the storm.

☸ Cultivate equanimity and drop your goals for lovemaking. Focus on shared intimacy and pleasure and "good enough sex."

CHAPTER 11

Loving Concentration
Tantric Meditation
and Orgasmic Bliss

You long for amazing sexual experiences. But are you cultivating the one thing that can create the conditions for transcendent sex? I'm not talking about mastering a sex technique hidden in an esoteric how-to manual or creating the perfectly seductive, sensual, bawdy boudoir. I'm talking about the mind state that is necessary for physical and emotional orgasmic bliss. If you wish to unleash your sexual potential, you need to be able to concentrate. Also called "attention" or "absorption," concentration is a state of focused mind. Concentration is single-pointed—that is, whatever you are paying attention to becomes the center, and even the totality, of awareness. Everything else—distracting thoughts, an itchy elbow—melts away. Whereas mindfulness has a broader, more mobile awareness to it—*I am mindful of your hand on my back, the jazz in the background, and how turned on I feel as we kiss*—concentration is a deep absorption into nothing but the sensation of your lips on mine. If you become deeply concentrated in meditation, you can even enter into profound, thought-free bliss states called *jhanas*. Your mind and body slow to the point where nothing seems to exist except for the meditation object. There is nothing but breath or lips—the meditator dissolves into the meditation. The sense of self and other disappear. There is no sense of "me, meditating" or "us, kissing" but rather a sense of open, connected, blissful oneness. And it feels fantastic.

Imagine experiencing single-pointed concentration and bliss when touching your partner's hair or making love, all distractions fading away as you become fully absorbed. Imagine the joy as the separate sense of "me" and "you" disappears and you melt into each other as one. Yet the ability to deeply concentrate is not common. The human mind developed to keep us safe, and it does so by scanning the environment with selective and rapidly alternating attention, as neuroscientist and Buddhist teacher Culadasa points out. So, unless you develop your concentration muscle, your mind will be easily distracted and unable to fall into the bliss of deep absorption.

And it's not all about bliss, either. Jhanic absorptions are great, but even on a regular level, if you are not paying attention, you are not fully living. Likely, you crawl out of bed, "do" your morning routine, then head out the door to work and errands and lunch and meetings, and then you arrive at home. Your spouse greets you warmly. You eat and talk about your day; you watch some TV; you go to bed. Was it an enlightened day? Did you really live it? Were you present, interested, curious, and aware? How many things did you miss today because you forgot to pay close attention? Whether you are stuck on a bus on your commute gazing at the ocean in rapture or listening closely to what your spouse is saying, loving concentration is about living and loving with focus and fullness—squeezing everything out of this one simple moment in time.

Let's explore bringing loving concentration to your sexual relationship. Recall that when you slow down and deeply focus on eating a raisin, your senses blaze with intensity. That single bite of a single raisin—when your mind is concentrated—imbues your whole being with sensual and emotional pleasure. When you listen with focused attention to a beautiful piece of music, you become one with the cello. Bliss and pleasure are enhanced by presence. Imagine making love that way. You sharpen your focus, and the intensity of this touch or kiss seems to increase, but really what has changed is your attention. As you concentrate on just-this-now, the now becomes the full experience. Concentration can lead to unified mind, sensory intensity, blissful orgasm, and tantric union. When you attend with deep concentration to your beloved, to this very touch, to the feelings of love and openness between you, to the sexual pleasure, you are practicing the ultimate in mindful loving—just by paying attention.

Slow Sex

My root teacher Namgyal Rinpoche used to say, "First, slow the mind. Then, wake it up." All new meditators know what he is referring to here. It is very difficult to concentrate when you are rushing around. If you want to train your mind in deep, single-pointed meditation, you need to slow down. Hence the slow, silent pace of meditation retreats. This concentration teaching applies to making love, too. Sex educator and author Nicole Daedone (2011), who teaches a sensation-specific type of slow, focused clitoral stroking she dubs "orgasmic meditation," says, "You cannot have great sex without sustainable attention. Attention is the special sauce. Attention makes sex exponentially better." If you are interested in really experiencing sexual bliss, you need to slow down, concentrate on sensation, and get truly in touch with touch. And one way to do this is by practicing slow sex.

Mindful sex, which we discussed in chapter 9, emphasizes *slowing the mind*. Slow sex, on the other hand, emphasizes *slowing the physical pace of lovemaking* so you can place concentrated focus on each sensation. How does your mouth on my nipple actually feel? Let's linger here—maybe for fifteen minutes—and find out. Perhaps the best way to understand slow sex is in comparison to regular sex. In a typical sexual encounter, the purpose is to reach a goal—usually orgasm. If the goal is missed, the sex—and the lover—is considered a failure. There is often an emphasis on more and bigger stimulation—this might mean harder, faster, deeper; pornography; or extreme sexual postures. Now don't get me wrong—there is nothing inherently wrong with enjoying intense stimulation. However, if you *need* intensity to feel, you are missing the profound sensuality that is available in your body. You may have become deadened to the pleasure and joy of the subtle—you are gobbling a handful of raisins but not really tasting anything. That's where slow sex comes in.

Slow sex is not linear or future focused. It is goalless sex—intuitive, here-and-now, open to possibilities, and free of expectations. It applies the enlightenment factors of concentration, tranquility, and equanimity to touch and receiving touch. Lovers are encouraged to explore each other with fresh bodies and minds in the present moment. The truth of impermanence reminds us that everything changes, including sex. Slow sex embraces that truth and allows the sensual experience to unfold, new and different each and every time. And slow sex is all about sensation. By touching, kissing, and penetrating at a slow pace, you begin to experience bare sensation, and to find it blissful—in fact, far more intense and blissful than the most overtly intense harder-faster-deeper sex you've had so far.

To practice slow sex, you slow down in some specific ways—concentrating on the bare experience of each sensation for some time. You may discover that you are not nearly as aware of sensation during sex as you think you are. If so, what a delightful discovery. It's as though your taste buds had been frozen for a year and then suddenly they thaw out. You are dazzled by the explosion of flavor that's been waiting within that strawberry all along. Slow sex can unfreeze your nerve endings and unleash the profound variety of sensory stimulation your body contains. That which you may have been deadened to—the joy of sensual pleasure—can blaze to life once again. Be patient, though. This slow sex sensation exploration can be challenging if you have not developed some ballast in your meditation practice. Happily, concentration is a skill that can be trained and developed. Your meditation cushion is actually a sex toy.

LOVE SKILL: Sexual Sensations Awareness and Naming

For this exercise, you will explore sensual touch with your partner with an emphasis on slowing the pace and concentrating on the bare experience of the sensation by naming what you feel. Begin by lying naked and taking some grounding breaths together. If your mind wanders into the past or the future, gently bring it back. You want to develop present-moment focus. Then, once your concentration is gathered, begin to focus intently on the sensations of touch—being touched and giving touch slowly. This is similar to the previous exploration. But now, to help sharpen your concentration, start naming the sensations. For example, "I feel my heart beating—it is slow and deep and fluttery all at the same time." "The feeling of your fingers brushing my back is tingly and electric and pleasant." "I feel my penis starting to grow harder; there is a tautness, a plump and achy delicious sensation." Notice, feel, inhabit, and then name the sensation. Drop all ideas of how you expect it to feel or memories of how touch usually feels, and discover this sensation, right now. Whenever you notice your attention has wandered, refocus and begin again, choosing one physical sensation that is happening presently. How do your genitals feel? Is there warmth, throbbing, or pulsing? Is the sensation pleasant, neutral, or unpleasant? Name that. Drop all expectations and pretend you are in this body for the first time. What would this touch feel like if you'd never been touched before? Continue naming the sensations and practice deep listening as your partner names their sensations. Experience, with curiosity, whether or not the naming practice helps you concentrate. If it does, continue to play with it during lovemaking.

Tantra for Dummies

So, what is Tantric sex, anyway? And why would you practice it? Tantra is a Sanskrit word that means "woven together" or "expansion through awareness," among other things. The word has been co-opted to refer to sexual Tantra as an act—you do tantric sex to get mind-blowing orgasms. That is not the form I am introducing here. In true Tantra, sex is energy, not activity. It is an enlightenment teaching, not a lust teaching. Tantric sensuality is about being in relationship with the energy within you, within your partner, and between the two of you. Tantra brings together meditative awareness and sexual pleasure for a deeper purpose.

Okay, but I know you want to hear about the sex, not just the enlightenment. Buddhist sexual Tantra is a form of sacred sexuality in which a couple shares slow, nonorgasmic intercourse as a prelude to bliss and insight. This type of lovemaking is therefore very different from blindly chasing after a pleasure state, then crashing, and then doing it all over again. Some features of tantric sexuality include using eye contact, touch, breath, and sound to quiet the mind and activate the sexual energy. The sexual energy is then exchanged between the lovers and directed into various places in the body. It is as though traditional sex is a firecracker—it is lit, it builds quickly in intensity, and then it pops. Tantric sex is like a controlled burn, a fire that is carefully laid, fanned into flames, and then the heat is played with—the tiny flame becomes a raging bonfire, but the bonfire is controlled, and the heat can be aroused, gentled, focused, or diffused at the will of the fire master. And the heat is not an end in and of itself. The heat and power are harnessed for a higher purpose, that of heightened states of bliss consciousness and profound sexual and emotional merging.

There is a great deal of power bound up in your sexuality. If you want to feel a glimpse of that power, try clenching your genitals and anus right now, as you read these lines. Likely you feel a tingle or movement or rush of sensation. These may not be sexual sensations of horniness, but they do have power. Feel the energy available to you—the energy you are literally sitting on. In traditional sex, that energy is stimulated and then quickly released in a climax orgasm. But what happens when you harness the fire, sustaining your energy instead of blowing it? Well, the gentlest touch can cause you to explode with pleasure and concentrated mind bliss. On my second date with my partner, we met at a tearoom for lunch. Suddenly he leaned across the table and kissed me, deeply, for the first time. My whole body began to gently shake with pleasurable energy. The fire had been stoked—not just by the kiss itself, but by the energy compatibility between us. I'd never felt that much full-body intensity from a kiss. So of course, I said yes to the third date.

Tantric sexual exploration can create a deep consciousness, love, pleasure, and intimacy between you and your beloved. So even if you are not yet ready for enlightenment, Tantra can still enhance your relationship in many ways, creating a depth and breadth to your mindful loving. Now, if you balk at the idea of avoiding orgasm, take heart—these practices can help you develop sexual ecstasy far beyond that of a typical orgasm. Instead of just saying, "Oh, God," at the point of orgasm, perhaps you will actually merge with Buddha nature. It gives the term "second coming" a whole new meaning. Tantric sex is an erotic practice that you and your partner can explore. But remember, the purpose is to open your awareness and your heart, not to win an Olympic medal for carnal gymnastics.

MINDFUL SKILL: Tantric Breathing Practices

Breathing together connects you with your partner and helps the energies of body and mind resonate in a powerful and loving exchange. Practice this with clothes on or naked. Sit facing your partner. If possible, sit cross-legged with your spine straight and your posture open and alert, yet relaxed. Get as close as possible, and make sure you are touching knees. Gaze deeply into each other's eyes and bring your attention to your breathing. At first, simply be together, breathing and connecting. Then, begin to synchronize your breath. Breathe in together at the same time; breathe out together. You can place a touch of a smile on your lips—this relaxes your mind and deepens concentration. Stay with this *synchronized breath* practice for a few moments, at first with your eyes open, and then explore it with your eyes closed.

Can you sense your partner's breath energy? Can you use a gentle touch to signal the pace of the mutual breath? Feel the distractions settle as you focus on breath and sensing your body and your partner.

Next, move on to *breath exchange*. Here, you inhale when your partner exhales, and then exhale when your partner inhales. Imagine you are exchanging life energy and loving kindness when you inhale your partner's breath and then exhale your breath into them. You may wish to explore connecting your palms together as you exchange breath or placing your palms on each other's heart.

The third breath practice goes by various names but is essentially a *circular tantric breath*. Still facing each other, place your attention at your root, or sexual, chakra. This energy gathering place is found in the area of the perineum—between the vaginal opening and anus for a woman, between the base of the scrotum and the anus for a man. Try tightening this area to get a feel for it. Then, as you inhale, imagine energy rising up from this root center, traveling up your spine, though your heart center, and up through the forehead to the crown of your head. On the exhale, reverse the flow, imagining breath and energy flooding down your body from the crown of your head through your forehead, throat, heart, belly, and to the sexual center. Once this flow is established, imagine the energy as a circle—flowing up from the root chakra on the inhale, curving through the crown, flowing down on the exhale, curving through the root chakra. Picture this as a loop of shining white light energy. Then, when you are ready, picture tracing a loop up through your own body on the inhale, then the light energy leaving your crown and entering your partner's crown, and then flowing down through your partner on the exhale. Concentrate on the energy sensations. Feel your way into, or imagine, your partner's experience. Gently allow the separation between you to blur as you breathe each other.

Beyond Climax: Multiple and Extended Orgasms

Did you know that a typical orgasm lasts an average of seven seconds for men and twenty seconds for women? Okay, sisters, let's have a little celebration about our higher number. But still, that is a pretty puny piece of pleasure. Imagine if you could experience the bliss of orgasm over and over, for minutes or even hours—would you be interested? I know I am. And I have good news. Multiple and extended orgasms are possible for both women and men. As far as I'm concerned, if we settle for a few seconds of bliss, we are underachievers. So how can you become more blissfully orgasmic?

It may be helpful to review the four-phase physiological sexual-response cycle. Imagine a scale from 0 to 10, 0 being not horny at all and 10 being climax. In phase one, *excitement*, you become turned on via mental desire or physiological arousal and move from 0 arousal to an arousal level of 1 or 2 out of 10. Your body is getting sexually excited. In phase two, *plateau*, you engage in physical sexual activity alone or with a partner. The body becomes more aroused—erection for males, lubrication and engorgement for females, increased heart rate, and many other physical signs occur—with concomitant sensations of pleasure. Think of this phase as your lovemaking phase. Arousal moves from 1 or 2 out of 10 to 7 or 8. By increasing and decreasing your sexual stimulation, you can move back and forth and up and down this arousal scale. Phase three is traditional *orgasm* or *climax*, muscle spasms and pleasure. Phase four, *resolution*, is the aftermath of orgasm. Accelerated body sensations slowly return to baseline. Climax is followed by physical and neurochemical changes that for many people lead to a sense of psychological letdown. At this point, men enter a *refractory period*—after ejaculation, they are not able to immediately achieve erection or climax again. Women, however, do not have a refractory period and may have more than one orgasm—they climax at 10, then dip down to 9, come back to 10 and climax again in a multiple orgasm. Yum.

So, stop settling for a few seconds of fun. Let's redefine what orgasm means to you and your lover.

In general parlance, "orgasm" means climax—that heightened, but fleeting, state of pleasure caused by involuntary muscle contractions that last for a few seconds. But for the purpose of Tantra, I'd like to expand the definition of orgasm. Think of orgasm as an ongoing process, not a culmination or end point. Tantric orgasm can be thought of as a flow state of pleasure. It is an undulating, ongoing experience of physical pleasure, emotional awareness, relational connection, and meditative or spiritual experience. It has no defined beginning, end, or time limit. Now, the implications for this redefinition of orgasm are pretty provocative. Instead of the traditional quick climax, you can develop an extended deep, slow, long-lasting orgasm with multiple peaks and valleys of erotic intensity. You can experience full-body orgasm and multiple orgasms. By training in loving concentration—single-pointed, undistracted focus that leads to a sense of merging with your partner—your mind and body can rest in the enlightenment factor of bliss and rapture. One definition of rapture is to be carried off to another sphere of existence. In Dharma terms, the thing that is carried off is your conceptual mind, as thinking dissolves into the open awareness of bliss and loving compassion. The entire experience of making love becomes orgasmic. And you can learn to hang out there, in bliss and conscious connection, together.

LOVE SKILL: Conscious Climax

It takes an awakened lover to stay present with their partner while they experience an orgasm. By now you've developed some skills in staying present with this moment even when it is intense. So, I invite you to practice conscious orgasm. Whether you are making love in your typical manner, having a quickie before work, or practicing Tantra, explore focusing your mind on the physical, emotional, and energetic sensations at orgasm. Show up right here, right now, in this erotic encounter. Don't escape into your own mind, shutting the door to your partner. Fantasy dilutes the intensity of the experience. Instead of leaving, focus your mind fully on this touch, this shared breath, this exchange with your beloved, and this sexual bliss. You will experience sensual intensity far beyond the typical climax that you've been settling for. Remember, there is an explosion of flavor in a single raisin, if you simply focus on it. So, learn to train and ride the stallion of your mind. Apply everything you've cultivated in your meditation practice to this erotic encounter for the most intense sensory experience of your life.

To practice conscious climax, stay connected with your lover, making eye contact and sharing breath as you approach orgasm. Just before the peak, focus on the impending waves of pleasure. As the orgasm waves begin to move through your lower body, stay present. Allow everything else to fall away except for your eye contact, your breathing, and your beating hearts. Instead of swooning into your own experience, share your orgasm with them, and receive their orgasm when they share it with you. Orgasm is an opportunity for profound sexual and emotional merging. Cultivate and sustain the energy as much as you are able. Allow the sense of separateness to dissolve. Send the bliss from your eyes to their eyes, from your heart to their heart. And smile.

Riding the Sexual Response Cycle

In a typical "nipple nipple crotch good-night" encounter, you may climb from 0 arousal to high arousal in a quick and linear fashion, climax, and then fall asleep. But if you are interested in becoming an orgasm maestro, learn to play the sexual response cycle like a cello.

Because multiple orgasms can be cultivated *for men as well as women*. It's true that after ejaculation, a man cannot come again for a while. However, if he separates orgasm from physical climax, the orgasm energy and sensation can be cultivated and repeated. This is very good news for the guys (and their partners). Men can have something that is the equivalent of a multiple orgasm. By utilizing tantric techniques, he brings his level of pleasure and arousal up to an 8 or 9 out of 10, and experiences the deep sensations of orgasm *without ejaculating*, which means he doesn't have the physical refractory period. He can then experience another wave of orgasmic bliss, then another. This is possible. It takes training, and an in-depth teaching of those techniques is out of the scope of this book, but you can check http://www.drcherylfraser.com for more tantric teachings.

Frankly, if you try to create multiple orgasms without the foundation of a calm, concentrated mind and a deep mindfulness of your sexual sensations, you won't get too far. But in time, you can go all the way, over and over again. You can learn to ride the sexual response cycle, exploring a rising and falling pattern of sexual arousal and pleasure from 1 to 9 in intensity without finishing with a 10 out of 10 climax. In traditional sex therapy terms, you are lingering in the plateau phase of arousal, moving up and down the scale. In tantric or slow sex terms, you are playing with sexual and mind energy, exploring the depth, breadth, and variety of prolonged erotic pleasure without pushing for a traditional orgasm.

Here is where things get even more interesting. As you become more proficient at these tantric practices, you can develop the ability for extended orgasm. For both women and men, this is a variation on multiple orgasm. Multiple orgasm feels like repeating waves of climax-like pleasure in the genitals. Extended orgasm is more of an ongoing, lingering, intense whole-body sensual and emotional bliss that happens when you remain at a peak of ecstatic pleasure without actually "coming." It is a deep, gentle, diffuse, full body-and-mind orgasmic sensation than a single or multiple climax orgasm. And it feels really, really great both sexually and emotionally.

In order to train in the art of erotic mindful loving, remind yourself that the aim is not to get to a climax orgasm, but rather to fully immerse in your own and your partner's sexual pleasure while simultaneously connecting deeply at an emotional, intimate level. When you practice remaining at a heightened state of pleasure and arousal without a climax orgasm, you develop control of your orgasmic response. Simply put, men can stay hard for hours, and both women and men can experience orgasmic bliss in the genitals or throughout the whole body with wave after wave of orgasmic pleasure. But unless you become adept at riding the sexual response cycle without climaxing, you will tend to come too early in the process, and you'll miss out on all that bliss. It's a bit like gobbling a fast food burger instead of luxuriating over a gourmet meal. Your body is trained to reach a pleasure level of about 7 out of 10 and then rapidly and predictably race through 8 and 9 to 10. This is sometimes called the "point of no return"—once you hit about a 7 of pleasure, it's too late to stop, and you quickly orgasm. First, practice until you are adept at reaching a 7 and then pulling back and calming your sexual excitement to a 4 or 5, and then building and then pulling back again. Only then are you ready to explore multiple, extended, and full-body tantric orgasm techniques and experience enlightened sex. So, learn to ride the sexual response cycle and put the OM into "Oh My."

LOVE SKILL: Prolonging Sexual Pleasure without Climax

For this exploration, you don't need any special skills. You will simply explore arousing yourself and your partner—going up and down in your arousal—without coming. Focus on conducting your erotic orchestra and staying within a 1 to 7 scale of arousal, dancing up and down. You can increase and decrease arousal solo or with your partner or, ideally, both. With masturbation, you can really focus on differentiating and harnessing your arousal by asking: When am I very close to climax but can pull back and stay in the pre-climax phase? What are the sensory clues that I'm too close and have reached the point of no return? You can begin to train yourself to stay at a level of heightened sexual pleasure without coming. With partner sex, make your usual lovemaking moves, just stop before climax. You can make a game of it—whoever climaxes loses this round. Who can hold out the longest? For this nonorgasmic lovemaking, you can bring in any of the techniques you have explored so far—you may wish to begin with erotic kissing, then some tantric breathing, and then sensory awareness of touch. Or you may jump in to your usual sexual routine but add the erotic restriction of no orgasm. How much fun can your sex be if you take your eye off the typical prize and playfully explore new eroticism together?

When you make love without orgasm, you will naturally find yourself bringing more curiosity and variety to your shared experience—after all, you have all that time to fill now that "nipple nipple crotch good-night" is off the table. You may kiss for longer, explore bodies more creatively, or switch sexual positions. The various Buddhist, Hindu, and Taoist tantric sex guides describe hundreds of varieties of sensual contact, from licking kisses to biting kisses to sucking on the lower lip, from scratching and tickling to whisper-light touch, from eye gazing to making erotic sounds to chanting mantra, from multiple ways to orally worship the genitals to energy exchange between two entwined but perfectly still bodies, from acrobatic yogic penetrative postures to the gentlest rocking in each other's laps. Explore pleasure in as many ways as you can imagine. Let go of expectations. Learn to please and be pleased in new ways, as though you have never made love before and do not know how to do it. And please, remember the factors of enlightenment and bring curiosity, joy, and energy to this beautiful, extended, for-play.

MINDFUL SKILL: Tantric Lovemaking 101

For this practice, you will focus on harnessing your sexual energy and practice moving it through your body so you can transform it into bliss and connection with your lover. Begin by connecting with gaze, breath, and slow sensation awareness touching. Open your heart. Treasure your beloved, and this very moment, as you trace their skin with today's fingertips, honoring their mind, their heart, and their body. Then move slowly and mindfully into focused, joyful lovemaking. Make love facing your partner, with one of you on top or both of you lying on your sides or, if you are limber, in the yab-yum posture (for heterosexual couples, the woman sits in the man's lap with her legs wrapped around the man's torso during penetration with the man seated cross-legged or with his legs extended out in front of him). Bring yourselves to a level of sexual excitement that is close to orgasm. Really experience the buildup of sensual energy, then experience it subside as you reduce the level of sexual stimulation. Then, when you are ready to explore harnessing and moving the energy in your body, follow these steps.

Rest at a high level of arousal and pleasure. Then imagine that all the sexual energy collects as a ball of light at the perineum or at the point of genital contact between you and your partner. Visualize a ball of white light, and imagine pouring all of the sensual and emotional pleasure and energy into that ball. Use your meditative concentration and mindfulness. You are practicing gathering and containing sexual bliss energy rather than rapidly releasing the energy through climax. At first, this practice might interrupt your arousal, and you may lose your sexual peak or erection. Don't be discouraged. You are exploring new ways of making love, and it makes sense that in the beginning, it may mess up your usual mojo.

Once you are able to rest at that height of arousal and imagine the ball of light at the base of your spine, refresh your connection with your partner with eye contact, a smile, a mutual breath, or by placing your hand on their heart. Your partner is also visualizing a light at their perineum or at the point of genital contact. Then, imagine pulling the light from the ball at the base of your spine up your spine and to your heart center. Rest your mind in the glowing light at the heart. Allow pleasure and connection to spread through your chest. Don't grasp or control. Relax and invite the light. Imagine your heart glowing more fiercely. Then begin to radiate the light out from your heart to your partner's heart. Experiment with moving the bliss energy, the light, the passion, the pleasure, back and forth between your hearts. You may want to gaze into each other's eyes or kiss deeply as you share the energy. What does it feel like to bank sexual energy instead of expel it, to move it through you, and to share it with your beloved? If you get lost, return to eye contact, mutual breath, or mindfulness of sensation. Let go of all striving and melt into the present experience. Melt your sense of self into the sense of oneness, of we, you and I as a whole, without separation. Melt into awakened love.

Love Bytes

♥ Loving concentration is a prerequisite for transcendent sensual bliss. It turns out your meditation cushion is a sex toy, and you can meditate your way to great sex.

♥ Slow sex is intuitive, nonlinear, goalless, exploratory, and focused on bare sensation. And bare sensation feels sensational.

♥ Typical orgasm—we can call it climax—lasts for a few seconds. Redefine orgasm as a flow state of pleasure, not an end point.

♥ Stay conscious at orgasm, remain present with your partner, and discover what shared orgasmic energy feels like.

Buddha Bytes

🪷 Awakened lovers can prolong their sexual pleasure without climax. They develop multiple, extended, and full-body orgasms.

🪷 You are sitting on a sexual powerhouse. Practice harnessing sexual bliss energy, moving it through your body, and sharing it with your beloved.

🪷 Ride the sexual response cycle and put the OM into "Oh My." Bring meditative concentration together with sensual pleasure.

🪷 Tantric sex is about exploring the energy within you and between you and can lead to sensory and emotional bliss far beyond typical sex.

Rewrite Your Love Story, Mindfully

Why did you pick up this book? Because somewhere deep in your longing you know that there is another way to be happy—that running after shiny objects doesn't bring fulfillment, that happiness and love come from within. It's as though there is a seed, or a bud, of wisdom in your belly that just wants to awaken, to be free from suffering. It started as a distant hope that maybe, just maybe, if you listened to the kitten scratching on your soul-door, you'd uncover the secret and unfold into the flower of awakened love. That bud is present in everyone—because the awakened state is the natural state, shining under the clouds. I haven't needed to bring anything to you. What I've shared with you are guidelines to help you uncover what is already present.

When your inner lover starts to wake up, to bloom, what happens? You begin to live and love from a place of flow. You cultivate that "in the moment" curiosity that leads to thrill and delight. You soothe your fears and move outside your comfort zone to explore emotional and sexual realms in ways that are, frankly, not explored by very many people. But this doesn't happen all by itself. So, as an awakened lover, you cultivate mindfulness. And why is mindfulness so important if you want to create a wonderful relationship? Mindfulness helps you be aware of things as they are so you can better focus on what matters and disregard what isn't important. As you become more aware, you know how you feel, what you are thinking, and how you want to act. Awareness is critical for emotional intelligence—how you recognize and work with your mind and emotions—and emotional intelligence is critical for deep relationship. After all, how can you dissolve irritation when you are not aware that you feel irritated? How can you guide your lover to touch your body in ways that make you shiver if you are not aware of the nuances of what feels pleasurable and what does not? How can you melt into transcendent bliss if your mind is distracted? And so you meditate, training your mind and liberating love.

Okay, but now what? Life is short. How do you want to live it? Well, if you are interested in being free from suffering, you want to live life with a peaceful mind and happy heart. And as an awakened lover, you want to experience life to the fullest with the one you love. The first step you took toward creating lifelong intimacy and sexual passion was to open *Buddha's Bedroom* and see what was inside. By applying the wisdom of the Buddha to your love relationship, you've made a choice to train your mind, take action in your love relationship, uncover the passion under the clouds of Marriage Inc., and awaken the lover within you. So, you've started walk the path of mindful loving and strengthen the three sides of your passion triangle—thrill, intimacy, and sensuality. As we approach the end of this book, I'd like say congratulations for committing to love and awakening. Thank you for trusting me and trusting yourself as you learn to uncover and become the passion you seek. Quite likely, you've had struggles and difficulties at some points along the way. You may have put the book down and then resumed the explorations months later. But you can always, in this moment, begin again. For this moment is always new, and passion is always present. And that is what *Buddha's Bedroom* is all about—loving right here, right now.

So where does the mindful loving path lead? It leads into your own mind and heart, where your potential for awakened love is uncovered. This love is then made manifest in your relationship, and together the two of you walk the path and become passion.

The Path of Mindful Loving—Are We There Yet?

Unless you feel madly in love with your mate at all times, never argue, and have a great sexual and emotional life, there is still more passion to become. By reading this book and exploring the love skills and mindful skills, you have embarked on a lifelong exploration. You've started to awaken the lover within you. But you know you are not there yet. So, consider the end of this book to be a beginning. Renew your intentions for love and passion. Commit the time and effort to training your mind and to cultivating the hobby of love and sex with your sweetheart. You have been introduced to tools and techniques, culminating with your passion plan, that will support you in your journey from this ending and into the beginning of the rest of your life as an awakened lover. Use the tools. Don't let them gather dust in the back of the passion toolshed. And remember, you are not alone. If you'd like to join a community of fledgling awakened lovers, you can find us at http://www.drcherylfraser.com. Join me live as I offer advanced teachings on sex and Buddhism, sign up to receive weekly email Love Bytes and Buddha Bytes, take the online Become Passion course, or attend a Buddha's Bedroom couples' retreat. Immerse yourself in the path of mindful loving. Take loving action and support yourself, your partner, and other couples on this profound journey of becoming an awakened lover—by learning to become passion.

LOVE SKILL: Your Passion Plan, Revisited

One great tool to support you moving forward is your passion plan. I suggest you make a date with your mate to review your plan every three months, revise it, and reboot your mindful loving. Here is what a sample passion plan looks like.

Passion Plan for Steven and Joleen

Thrill

Daily

Cuddle in the morning before we get out of bed. Make eye contact and say our daily vows.

Practice mindful loving meditation for twenty to thirty minutes.

Ask each other two interesting questions over dinner and allow ourselves to be surprised by each other.

Weekly

Spend ten minutes reviewing our passion triangle: How did we do this past week? How can we improve?

Review a difficult conversation and discuss what we were each expecting and hanging on to, and how we created our own unhappiness.

Set one loving intention for the week to come—one new relationship skill to practice and explore.

Monthly

On alternating months, we will each plan a novelty date—something fresh, exciting, and new—to dazzle each other.

Annually

We will go on a romantic vacation somewhere fascinating and pretend it is our first vacation together.

Intimacy

Daily

We will try to catch each other doing things right and point out the good instead of the bad.

Every time we see each other after time apart, even an hour, we will practice the three-breath hug.

We will touch before we talk and while we talk, particularly if it is a difficult conversation.

Weekly

We will talk about a disagreement using The Other Side of the Clock technique—listening to and validating each other.

We will practice the time-out when we need it and apologize and repair when we stumble.

We will practice meditating together on generosity, kindness, and compassion.

Monthly

We will review how our hobby—our lover life—is doing. Then we will devote a whole day to playing together—doing something fun that brings us closer.

Annually

We will enroll in a couples course or weekend love workshop so we can learn and grow as awakened lovers.

Sensuality

Daily

We will kiss each other good-bye with passion and with tongue.

We will shower naked and tease each other's body in a sensual way.

We will share an erotic love note, text, or whisper.

Weekly

We will make love at least twice a week. If we are not in the mood, we will cultivate our desire and arousal alone or together.

We will spend one hour a week giving each other a sensual massage and exploring sensual touch deeply.

We will spend an afternoon exploring and learning about tantric energy, conscious orgasm, or full-body orgasm.

Monthly

We will cash in a sensual IOU and have a dark sensual energy date where we explore an erotic, sexy taboo. We will take turns planning this for each other.

Annually

We will plan an erotic weekend—perhaps taking a tantric sex course or having a naked weekend at a cabin.

Your Awakened Lover Journey

I believe the Buddha would agree that becoming passion is a good start on the path to enlightenment. Because once you let go of expecting your lover to make you happy, you are well on the way to loving without selfishness and fear. As you become passion, you become compassionate. Awakened lovers put their partner's well-being far ahead of their own. This is how you sustain your passionate, intimate, thrilling, exciting, sexy connection. The more you practice mindful loving and the more you practice meditation, the more natural it will feel to think of your sweetheart before you think of yourself.

But what about life beyond the bedroom? The true path to happiness is to serve others, not yourself. As your compassion grows, the hobby of loving becomes a life mission—you take your loving view into loving action not just with your partner, but with everyone. Mindful loving is about compassion and awareness, whether you are making love with your partner or making love with the world. As your ego softens and you seek to understand others, you see that they too want happiness. You feel more connected, kind, and curious.

Yes, I hope this work helps you be a better lover. But let's use it to also make us better people. Together, let's work on awakening the planet, one lover at a time. Because that's the ultimate purpose of *Buddha's Bedroom*. And if along the way to awakening the world, you create a passionate sex life, laugh with delight and dance like a teenager, communicate like a master, and your eyes light up when your sweetie of five months or fifty years walks through the door, love is being made manifest. So, take your next step to awakening as a lover, and make the world a better place, both in bed and out. There are many more miles to this journey, and not all of them will be easy. But by slowing down and becoming mindful, you create the opportunity to become passion, over and over again. The path of mindful loving has no end. It is an endless exploration, a lifelong study, until death do you part. No matter what state your relationship is in at this very moment, take a breath. Then choose to begin again. Rewrite your love story, mindfully.

Acknowledgments

Homage to my Dharma teachers, the women and men who have pointed the way to the path of awakening. Thank you to my root teacher, Namgyal Rinpoche, who called me an idiot for spending life energy on helping people decorate their prisons, instead of showing them that the doorway to liberation is always wide open. Thank you to Lama Mark Webber for boundless teachings and for telling me that love relationship is an important part of the path of enlightenment. Thank you also to Ontul Rinpoche, Chokyie Nyima Rinpoche, Culadasa, Adrienne Ross, Phillip Moffit, Trudy Goodman, and Jack Kornfield for profound Dharma. And an extra shout out to Trudy, who when I said, "I used to teach sex, now I only teach Dharma," replied, "Why not teach both?" and who has supported this work from the beginning. And to all faces and forms of White Tara, thank you for inspiration, nurturing, and wisdom.

To the women and men who have guided me along the path of psychology and sex therapy, in journeys both inner and outer, professional and personal, thank you. In particular, gratitude to Jim Marcia, Bob Ley, Pam Duncan, Ron DeStefano, Lori Brotto, John and Julie Gottman, Michael Barden, Alexandra Hunter, and Dirk Evers.

At New Harbinger, special thanks to Ryan Buresh, who read my column in *Mindful* on making your love life a hobby and immediately asked me if I'd thought of writing a book. My answer was yes. And here it is. Thanks also to Gretel Hakanson and Caleb Beckwith for editorial support, to Amy Shoup for the cover design, and to the marketing teams at New Harbinger and Raincoast books. It's been a pleasure to work with such a talented group of passionate people.

To all the couples who have had the courage to embark on the path of mindful loving and who have shared their intimate lives with me on my psychology couch, in weekend workshops, and through online courses, I honor your wisdom and celebrate the love and passion you have uncovered. Thank you for teaching me and trusting me to teach you.

To the men I have loved and to the men who have loved me, sometimes at the same time, thank you for helping me kill the soulmate.

And to Richard, for choosing to hold hands with me within the sea of impermanence while we manifest love, passion, and awakening—let's keep getting naked in both body and mind, until death do us part, and beyond.

References

Basson, Rosemary. 2000. "The Female Sexual Response: A Different Model." *Journal of Sex and Marital Therapy* 26(1): 51–65.

Brotto, Lori A. 2018. *Better Sex Through Mindfulness: How Women Can Cultivate Desire.* Vancouver, BC: Greystone Books.

Brotto, Lori A., and M. Barker (Eds.). 2014. *Mindfulness in Sexual and Relationship Therapy.* New York: Routledge.

Culadasa (J. Y.) and M. Immergut with Jeremy Graves. 2015. *The Mind Illuminated: A Complete Meditation Guide Integrating Buddhist Wisdom and Brain Science for Greater Mindfulness.* Pearce, AZ: Dharma Treasure Press.

Daedone, Nicole. 2011. *Slow Sex: The Art and Craft of the Female Orgasm.* New York: Grand Central Life and Style.

Gottman, J. M., and N. Silver. 2015. *The Seven Principles for Making Marriage Work: A Practical Guide from the Country's Foremost Relationship Expert,* 2nd Edition. New York: Harmony Books.

Hertenstein, M. J., R. Holmes, M. McCullough, and D. Keltner. 2009. "The Communication of Emotion via Touch." *Emotion* 9(4), 566–573.

Masters, W. H., and V. E. Johnson. 1980. *Human Sexual Response.* New York: Bantam.

McCarthy, B., and E. McCarthy. 2012. *Sexual Awareness,* 5th Edition. New York: Routledge.

Metz, M. E., and B. W. McCarthy. 2007. "The 'Good-Enough Sex' Model for Couple Sexual Satisfaction." *Sexual and Relationship Therapy* 22(3): 351–362.

Perel, E. 2006. *Mating in Captivity: Unlocking Erotic Intelligence.* New York: HarperCollins.

Sharp, frank, and fearless, **Cheryl Fraser, PhD**, is a Buddhist psychologist and sought-after relationship expert. She has helped thousands of couples jump-start their love life and create passion that lasts a lifetime.

A highly successful and awarded Fulbright scholar, she has conducted extensive research on sexual behavior and what causes love relationships to succeed or fail. With her groundwork, she created the *Become Passion* online workshop for couples. She has a thriving private practice in sex and couples therapy.

A former talk radio host, Cheryl is a dynamic guest expert for television and radio, appearing on multiple programs, including *The Experts*, CBC *Marketplace*, *Air America*, the *Loving Well* podcast, and many more.

As a columnist for *Mindful* and *Best Health* magazines, Cheryl explores love, sex, relationships, and the human experience. Her approach to life and to helping others is based in her practice of meditation and Buddhism, which she has studied for twenty-five years in both the Tibetan and Theravaden traditions. She was given permission to teach by her root teacher Namgyal Rinpoche, and she is resident meditation teacher for Island Dharma. Her work is encapsulated in the teaching of *Mindful Loving*, where she brings the Buddha's teachings into the bedroom.

When Cheryl is not in India, Tibet, or at a three-month silent Buddhist meditation retreat, she lives on Vancouver Island, BC, Canada, with her man and their menagerie, practicing the passion she preaches.

www.drcherylfraser.com

Foreword writer **Jack Kornfield, PhD**, is cofounder of the Insight Meditation Society in Barre, MA, and a founding teacher at Spirit Rock Meditation Center in Woodacre, CA. He is author of many books, including *A Path with Heart* and *The Wise Heart*.

Foreword writer **Trudy Goodman, PhD**, is a senior Vipassana teacher in Los Angeles, CA; cofounder of the Growing Spirit program; and contributing author to several books, including *Wisdom and Compassion in Psychotherapy*, *Clinical Handbook of Mindfulness*, and *Mindfulness and Psychotherapy*.

MORE BOOKS for the SPIRITUAL SEEKER

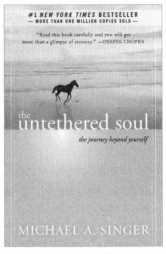